AUSCHWITZ

AUSCHWITZ

TRUE TALES FROM A

GROTESQUE LAND

SARA NOMBERG-PRZYTYK

Translated by Roslyn Hirsch

Edited by Eli Pfefferkorn and David H. Hirsch

The University of North Carolina Press

Chapel Hill and London

© 1985 The University of North Carolina Press

All rights reserved

Manufactured in the United States of America

11   10   09   08   07   18   17   16   15   14

Library of Congress Cataloging in Publication Data

Nomberg-Przytyk, Sara, 1915–

Auschwitz: true tales from a grotesque land

Translated from the unpublished Polish manuscript.

1. Auschwitz (Poland: Concentration camp)   2. Holocaust, Jewish (1939–1945) — Poland — Personal narratives.

3. Nomberg-Przytyk, Sara, 1915– .   I. Hirsch, Roslyn.

II. Title.

D805.P7N6   1985   940.53'15'0392404386   84-17386

ISBN 978-0-8078-1629-5

ISBN 978-0-8078-4160-0 (pbk.)

To my grandson
Sasha Przytyk

The editors and the translator would like to thank the Sigmund Strochlitz Foundation, which gave its support to this project in memory of Herman and Regina Strochlitz, two of the six million.

CONTENTS

TRANSLATOR'S FOREWORD

he original Polish typescript of this book, dated 1966, is on deposit in the Yad Vashem Archive, where it was discovered by Eli Pfefferkorn. When I first undertook to translate a forty-page segment of typescript, supported by a generous grant from Mr. Sigmund Strochlitz, I knew nothing about the author, not even whether she was still alive. It took no more than a few minutes of reading for me to recognize that I was dealing with an author of unusual talent. It was not that the manuscript broke new ground on the general nature of the Auschwitz-Birkenau death factory, for by the time I started translating, in September 1981, the horrors had already been documented many times over. What struck me about this manuscript was the author's ability to make the characters in the camp emerge as unique individuals, even against the backdrop of camp depersonalization and imminent extermination. Here was a readable, dramatically compelling account, not simply of the author's consciousness, but of the people in the camp who were caught in the meatgrinder of history—not only prisoners but captors as well.

In May 1982, aided by a travel grant from the American Philosophical Society, I was able to go to Jerusalem and, with the kind assistance of Danuta Dombrowska and Shalmi Barmore of Yad Vashem, obtain a copy of the entire typescript of about two hundred pages. My next step, on returning to the United States, was to determine whether the manuscript had been published in any form. A check of the British Museum Catalogue and of the NUC of the Library of Congress revealed that a Sara Nomberg-Przytyk had published a book entitled *Columny Samsona* (*The Pillars of Samson*) in Lublin, Poland, in 1966. After obtaining one of the few copies available in this country, via interlibrary loan, I soon discovered that *The Pillars of Samson* narrated events in the Bialystok Ghetto up to the time of its liquidation, at which point the author had been transported to the Stutthof concentration camp. Since *Auschwitz: True Tales from a Grotesque Land* starts with the author's being transported from Stutthof to Auschwitz, and since the author mentions her experiences in the Bialystok Ghetto, I concluded that both books were by the same author. Although *Auschwitz* is so fast-paced that I needed no incentive other than the entire manuscript of the journal itself to continue with the translation, my discovery did heighten my sense of urgency.

By December 1982, I had completed translation of the entire manuscript, but I was still entirely at sea as to the fate and possible whereabouts of the author. It would have made sense, of course, to write to the Polish publisher of *The Pillars of Samson*, but the situation in Poland was not conducive to calling attention to an author who obviously had played a role in the political arena.

In late 1983, after the manuscript had been accepted for publication, Eli Pfefferkorn, now Holocaust Scholar Researcher of The U.S. Holocaust Memorial Council, learned that Sara might be living in Israel. Since Eli was planning a research trip to Israel at the time, locating Sara became his top priority. As it turned out, Sara was not in Israel but living in a small town in Canada, just north of the Vermont border.

Now that my husband and I have met with her and talked to her, thanks, in part, to a travel grant from the Brown Faculty Development Fund, awarded to my husband by Associate Provost James Patterson, I can fill in some of the lacunae in the provenance of the manuscript. Born on 10 September 1915, in Lublin, Poland, Sara was brought up in a hasidic atmosphere. Her grandfather, a well-known Talmudist in Poland, served as principal of a Yeshiva in Warsaw and subsequently as the rabbi of a small town outside Lublin. Many of Sara's relatives were rabbis.

Growing up in a Jewish neighborhood in Lublin, Sara knew what it meant to live in poverty. As a young girl she was deeply impressed by the sight of Jewish children dying of malnutrition and of women growing old prematurely. She herself was often sent home from school for lack of tuition money. On those occasions, a card was attached to her record specifying: "Sara Nomberg is not allowed to attend classes." At such times, Sara felt that she was suffering a grave injustice.

She recalls a childhood scene as follows:

We are children going on a picnic. Sitting on both sides of the wagon we are vibrant with a sense of joy and anticipation. The wagon comes to a clearing near a small village. The driver stops and sends us to the clearing, telling us to have fun. We run and play, frisking like young colts. Our shouts and singing bring the children from the nearby village, who stand at a distance, watching us as if we were dirt. One of them starts yelling, "Jews, scabs." The others join in. We feel icy hatred enveloping us. The driver gathers us and drives us away when the village youths start pelting us with stones. I keep asking myself questions that Jews must have asked themselves for thousands of years. "Where does this hate come from? Must it be this way?"

Eventually, Sara attended a *gymnasium* in Lublin and the University in Warsaw. Thanks to her strong sense of social justice, Sara spent five years in confinement as a political prisoner. When Germany invaded Poland in 1939, Sara fled toward the east. In 1941 she set out for Warsaw with some friends but finally decided to remain in Bialystok because she had taught in Bialystok before the war and had a wide circle of acquaintances there. From 1941 to August 1943, when the Germans made *Judenrein*, Sara survived in the Bialystok Ghetto. From Bialystok she was shipped to Stutthof, and from Stutthof to Auschwitz.

After her liberation she returned to Poland, where, in 1946, she was married to Andrzej Przytyk, a magistrate. She worked as a journalist in Lublin until October 1968, when, being forced to leave the country, she emigrated to Israel. In 1975 she left Israel to join the older of her two sons in Canada.

I was interested in knowing how her manuscript came to be deposited in the Yad Vashem Archive and why it was dated 1966, the same year of the publication of *The Pillars of Samson*. Sara informed me that the manuscript had been accepted for publication in Poland and was about to go to press when, in June 1967, she was called into the editor's office and told that, in the wake of the Six-Day War between Israel and the Arab states, her book could not be published until she removed all references to Jews. Sara argued that her narrative was not only about Jews but about people in Auschwitz, regardless of nationality, race, religion, or political persuasion. It would, she continued, be very strange indeed to present a narrative of Auschwitz that contained no mention of Jews at all. This argument fell on deaf ears, so Sara withdrew the manuscript and took it out of the country, clandestinely, when she left Poland. When she arrived in Israel, friends in the Lublin Society made the copy that was then deposited in the Archive.

Roslyn Hirsch

AUSCHWITZ

A L I E N A T I O N

I lay on the lowest bunk of a three-decker bed, wrapped in a blanket. I was not cold. I was not hungry. I had drunk enough cold water to quench my thirst. I had gotten rid of the lice. You might say that I felt happy. Around me people were asleep. A ray of hope crept into my heart. Maybe here, in Stutthof,* I would manage to last through the war. After three nights and three days of a terrible trip in a stifling, closed freight car, without food or water, we had stopped suddenly in a pine forest. A cold snow mixed with rain was falling, but the trees were green, and the leaves made a rustling noise. It had been two years since I last saw a tree. There were no trees in the ghetto and none in the Bialystok† prison, and maybe because of that their aroma and rustling struck me as being unusual.

On the very first evening I drank water—simple, cold water—from the sink. But I had been dreaming about one drop for three days and nights of travel in the closed freight car, during which time my tongue had dried out like a piece of leather. I kept hearing a terrible hum in my temples, and one thought kept going through my mind, that I might die before having had a drink of water. Right after our arrival, a Polish *kapo* from Poznan took us to the toilet, where there were sinks with running water. I could not tear myself away. It had a taste of heaven, and to this very day I can still feel that taste in my mouth. We were the first Jewish transport to arrive in Stutthof, a motley crew who shared nothing in common but the tragedy of having been born Jewish. No wonder we met with little sympathy from the other prisoners. Nobody

*Concentration camp about twenty miles east of Gdansk (Danzig) and three hundred miles north of Auschwitz, on the Baltic Sea, opened in September 1939. Survivors of the uprising in the Bialystok Ghetto were sent there in the summer and fall of 1943.
†An industrial city with a substantial Jewish population before World War II, on the Polish-Russian border. Bialystok was under German occupation from 15 to 22 September at which time it was ceded to the USSR. The Germans re-occupied the city from 27 June 1941 to 27 July 1944.

wanted any contact with us, and nobody asked us about anything. We were alienated. We felt that no one wanted us here. It was the isolation of the prisoners in the Jewish cell that had hurt me most of all in the Bialystok prison. The whole world was involved in a battle, but the prisoners in our cell were not a part of it. Why did no one make contact with us? I had asked that question in Bialystok and I could get no answer. Now the same thing was happening to us in Stutthof. We were put in a separate block and found ourselves in complete isolation.

A *blokowa* was appointed over us. It was Ania, a Jewish woman from Bialystok who was overflowing with energy. I cannot explain why the *kapo* gave her that job. But still, I was not too surprised, because I knew that Ania would always find a cushy position for herself. She treated us fairly, but at the same time, she always managed to reserve a warm and comfortable place to sleep and a plate of thick soup for herself and her darling Liza. Liza was ten years younger than Ania. Even in the Bialystok Ghetto I could not figure out why Ania displayed such maternal affection toward her. Ania fed her and dressed her; she did all the hard work for her. She was proud of Liza's beauty. Only in the camp was it possible to find such affection among women.

There were two hundred women of varying ages in our block. The oldest woman in our transport was eighty-eight years old, and the youngest was seventeen. Among the older women there were some who had absolutely no idea of what was happening or of where they were. From the first day, fights started breaking out over the silliest things: over a place in the food line, over a drink of water, over a potato in the soup. I listened to the bickering, and it was difficult for me to believe that these women had experienced the liquidation of the Bialystok Ghetto and the death of their dear ones.

The fight for food took on a horrible form. In order to make sure that they would have a supply of food, the women would hide some bread under their pillows at night. Then the next morning there would be fights over bread that women stole from under each other's pillows. They cried in desperation, yelled, and pounced at each other's eyes. Ania then decided to divide each day's portion of bread into three parts and to issue one part with each meal. That quieted things down for a while; every woman received her fair portion.

One morning Ania noticed that one loaf of bread was missing. The loaf was a daily portion for ten women. Ania divided the bread that was left into smaller portions. The next day another loaf of bread was missing. This time Ania told the women about the theft. A terrible fight broke out. I have to admit that this fight for a loaf of bread filled me with optimism. If they are still willing to fight for a piece of bread, if they still react like normal human beings, if they have not just given up on everything, that means that we are still alive. Again that ray of hope breaks through; maybe we will succeed in waiting out the end of the war here in Stutthof.

For the next few days, someone kept stealing the bread. I observed the women carefully. It was difficult for me to discover anything. One day Ania conducted a search. If there is someone stealing a loaf of bread every day, that person must be hiding it someplace. Unfortunately, the search brought no results. No bread was found.

It was a bright night. The moon glistened on the snow that had been falling for the last few days. At night I always trembled with fear. Everything was so senseless and terrible. All the doubts and questions that I suppressed during the day came to haunt me at night. Why did we not assemble for roll call like the other prisoners? Why did they not take us to work? They dressed us in Russian prison outfits. They gave us soup and bread. Was it possible that they would give us Jews food and not demand something in return? What was behind it all? As far as we were concerned, nothing pleasant, I was sure. The whole time that I was in Stutthof only once did an SS man, with the insignia on his sleeve, come into our block. He was young. He looked at us in disbelief, as though surprised to see that we were human beings, that we walked on legs, that we had faces with eyes in them. How he looked at us! It gave me goose pimples. Now, in the watches of the night, I still remember that look.

Suddenly my thoughts were interrupted by a scream. We all

jumped from our beds. A strange girl was standing at the closet
where the bread was kept. She was young and she wore stripes, so
she was not Jewish. Where had she come from? The gate was
locked from inside. The women tied her to a chair and stuffed her
mouth so she could not scream. We were afraid that her screaming might bring the SS men.

She was a Ukrainian who lived in the next block. At night she
would take the glass out of the window and climb inside. She
would take a loaf of bread, leave quietly, and replace the glass.

"Soon you are going to the gas, so what do you need the bread
for?" she asked.

The women wanted to hold her prisoner until morning, then
take her to the *kapo* and let her know what was going on. But we
came to the conclusion that this would not do us any good. It
would only make more enemies for us. We untied our night guest
and let her out the window. Her words had cast a deep chill over
us.

Christmas was approaching. It is difficult for me to say, right
now, who it was that had the idea of taking advantage of the holiday spirit to break the barriers dividing us from the other prisoners. Maybe we could "organize" some food, prepare a show, and
invite the *kapo* and other functionaries we came in contact with
every day. Our invitation was accepted, so we spent the whole
month of December getting ready to receive our guests.

On the first day of the holiday season, they came to us as though
they were ashamed of having let themselves be talked into coming. Ania, our *blokowa*, greeted them graciously and seated them
at a long table. We young ones started our program. We had decided to recite poems that would make clear to them our belief
that Poland was our fatherland and show them that we were ready
to give our lives for her. I had imagined that on this evening they
would tell us why we were so isolated. Would the answer be that
we were so persecuted and unfortunate?

Our words fell on deaf ears. We felt that we had not broken
through the wall of ill feeling and disdain, and that we could not
even succeed in raising a trace of compassion. That was how it
remained until Liza started singing a song about a Jewish mother,

and we, who had lost our mothers so cruelly, could not keep ourselves from crying. We wept quietly, not thinking much about our guests. Then the first *kapo* broke the silence, thanked Liza and all of us for the evening. She was moved. At the door she told us secretly that all the Jews would be leaving Stutthof in January. She did not mention our destination, but her expression did not presage any good.

EXCHANGE

The head of the Stutthof camp looked us over carefully as we were being prepared for the transport. Since he was accepting only Jews it was clear that the trip was bad news. Rumors were flying everywhere that we were being sent to Treblinka to be gassed. Others whispered that they would not take us very far. They would just take us into the forest and shoot us.

"Why are we being inspected like cattle?" we kept reflecting when they ordered us to march in pairs in front of the commandant's fat face. While we were in Stutthof we wore the uniforms of Russian prisoners of war, often dirty and full of holes. For the trip we were given winter uniforms, and the commandant was inspecting them to make sure that there were no holes and that all the buttons were sewed on.

"Where are we going? Why are they so concerned with our appearance?" How the rumor got started I do not know, but the story that was making the rounds was that we were going to be traded to the Russians in return for German prisoners. We all said, "Nonsense!" But deep down in our hearts we believed the rumor because we wanted to believe it.

Those who were remaining behind took their leave of us in different ways. Since we had spent barely two months here, we had not quite managed to grow into the life of the camp. Because we had lived in isolation in a separate block, we had not had an opportunity to make close contacts with the other prisoners. Isolation breeds alienation and even enmity, so when, one frosty January morning, we marched along the tracks, guarded by SS men, nobody gave us as much as a friendly smile.

We waited dejectedly for the train that would be taking us into the unknown. It was a long time before the train arrived. We made small talk about anything in order to keep our minds from the vexing thoughts of "Where are we going, to another camp or to the gas?"

Suddenly a train arrived on the tracks. It was empty. We did not move, thinking that surely this train could not be the one we were waiting for. We already knew what kind of trains they used to transport prisoners. We were greatly surprised when the SS man turned to us and politely told us to board the train. "They are mocking us," Liza whispered to me. "Soon they will chase us out of the train to the tune of shouts and blows."

We walked into the compartments. There was enough room so that everyone had a place to sit. "Maybe you want to sit near the window," Liza joked. In each compartment there was an SS man to guard us. The train started. We looked at each other and shrugged our shoulders. Unbelievable! We were traveling like normal people. We could take advantage of a wash basin, water, and a toilet. What's going on here? This is probably a new trick. "Maybe this road leads to Paradise," I thought. Everything was so unusual that we sat perfectly still, afraid that if we moved we might somehow burst the bubble. If none of this is true, if the terrible truth is going to break in on us at any moment, at least for this moment let us live in our dream. The words of a Yiddish song ran through my mind. "Suppose," the words go, "I build castles in the air. Suppose my dream will never come true. Still, dreaming is better, dreams are brighter." So we dreamed.

The silence in our compartment amazed even our guard. "Why are you sitting so quietly? You can talk. Sing," he told us magnanimously.

My first impulse was to question him. Maybe I could find out where we were going. But on second thought I just shrugged my shoulders. "Why throw dreams out the window?" Suddenly the door of our compartment opened and a second guard came in with food. Everybody was given a slice of bread, a piece of margarine, and a piece of cheese. "Eat this for supper. You will get more food tomorrow," he said and went on to the next compartment.

In Stutthof we had never received such food. If we were allowed some margarine with our bread that was the height of luxury. Now here we were getting cheese in addition to margarine. When I was being transported from Bialystok to the camp in Stutthof we did not even get a crumb of bread and not even a drop of water. Now we had just boarded the train and they were not only bringing us food but politely telling us about tomorrow's breakfast. What was going on? Perhaps in my dreams I had changed devils into angels. Our compartment continued in silence. We enjoyed the bread and the hope that timidly crept into our hearts.

I asked our escort if he would allow me to go into the next compartment. I wanted to talk and to hear what the others were saying about the situation. He gave me permission and I found that the next compartment was just as silent as ours. I sat down next to Genia, a pleasant, black-haired girl from Lodz. I knew that Genia was getting ready to run away. She told me in Stutthof that, as soon as an opportunity presented itself, she was going to take a chance. "After all, some people do succeed, so I am going to try," she had said the day before the transport. What had she decided now? Was she planning to run away? Clearly it would be easier from this kind of train than from a freight train with barred tiny windows. So here I was, sitting next to Genia, wondering what she was going to do.

"What do you say?" she asked right off the bat. "Do you know where they are taking us? Shall we run or not? Maybe it's true that we're going to be exchanged. If that's the case, why should I jump to my death? What do you think? What shall I do? Say something," she begged.

An exchange! What nonsense. How easily she had fallen into the dream.

"I will wait," she went on. "Maybe tomorrow the matter will clear up."

By this time darkness had fallen. We passed darkened train stations without stopping. On several occasions the train stopped and stood in the middle of a field for a long while. I could not figure out where we were going. We dozed. Someone talked in her sleep. Somebody sighed. Our escort slept with outstretched legs, his rifle between his knees.

I woke up in the middle of the night with a feeling of joy. I imagined that I heard a choir singing. At first I did not believe my own ears, but later I could even catch the words of the song. The women in the next compartment were singing. Maybe we should sing something, too. Let the worst happen tomorrow. Today we are going to the unknown, so let us sing. Timidly I started a Russian song about Katiusha. Everybody joined in, quietly at first, and then more loudly. The escort did not say a word.

At dawn we fell asleep, our faces still distorted with anxiety. When it was completely light again, more food was brought in, accompanied by a large thermos of hot coffee and a few cups, much to our surprise. Hot coffee during a trip from a camp! The head of our transport brought it in. I remember how he unbuttoned his military coat, sat down on the bench, and spread his legs wide as he took delight in our amazement.

"The coffee tastes good, doesn't it? Straight from the buffet."

He bowed his head and smiled with pleasure. We received a full day's ration of food: bread, margarine, cheese, and red sausage. The curtains were drawn across the window, and the SS man did not allow them to be opened.

"Why should the outside world know what kind of train it is?" he explained.

We continued to travel into the unknown. The length of the trip and the unusual treatment we were getting started to make our anxiety acute. Was there anything in our situation that could portend some good? During the day we stopped, often in the middle of nowhere. Sometimes the train stood motionless for a few hours, as though waiting for something. Was the track occupied? Clearly the SS men did not want us to know where we were going.

"We are probably close to the border," whispered an old hunchbacked lady who was traveling in the same compartment.

"To which border?" I asked. At first I did not realize what she was driving at.

"What do you think?" she answered. "We must be close to the spot where they are going to make the exchange."

I do not know why, but at that moment all my illusions left me. How could I have believed such nonsense even for a moment? Why had I not told Genia not to hesitate and to jump if she felt strong enough?

Meanwhile darkness fell again, and again we were given hot coffee. Now the train sped on quickly to our rendezvous with the worst. Now I could think about only one thing. How could I get to

Genia and tell her what I thought about the exchange? There was silence in the compartment. We said nothing to each other. What was there to say? Now that I had rid myself of my illusions, I saw the satanical smiles in the eyes of our escorts. When the commander of the transport asked if we wanted anything, I saw that our tormentors were toying with us.

Suddenly the silence of the night was shattered by German shouts and shooting. Only the SS men could bellow like that. Our commandant jumped out of his seat and pointed the barrel of his rifle in our direction. I needed no explanation to know what the shooting and the shouting meant. Genia had decided not to wait for the exchange. She jumped while the train was going at full speed. The Germans had not expected this. When they realized what had happened and started to shoot, the train was already far from the spot where she had jumped. I thought that after the escape the escorts would stop smiling at us. Nothing of the kind. Early the next morning we again received the food and hot coffee. But nothing could squelch our feeling of dread. It was starting to get dark when the train stopped. At that moment the devil in our escorts showed himself. *"Raus, raus, schneller"* ("Out, out, faster"), they shouted, smashing us across our heads with their rifles. The train had stopped next to a hill of gravel, down which we had to slide, injuring our arms, legs, and faces. Finally, we found ourselves at the bottom of the hill, facing a large building on which we saw a huge sign: "Auschwitz—Oswiecim." We had reached the border, all right, the border of Hell.

NEW ARRIVALS

At Auschwitz the *zugangi* (new arrivals) were at the bottom of the ladder. They were pariahs who were treated contemptuously by the other prisoners. They were beaten and kicked mercilessly and endlessly. They constantly tormented themselves over the orders and commands that were unfamiliar to them and that they could not understand. *Zugangi*—the new prisoners who did not know how to "organize"—did not know how or where to hide; they made themselves absurd trying to defend their human dignity. Just for fun the *sztubowa* would beat a new prisoner on the face for a long time, until the eyes looked as if they were blue "eyeglasses." The new inmate would be so surprised that she would not even shield her face and would look around innocently and ask: "Why are you hitting me? I am a human being."

The *sztubowa* would answer, "You are a *zugang*, a stinking *zugang*. For my part you can drop dead right now."

On 13 January 1944, I became a *zugang*, a stinking, hungry, battered outcast of a *zugang*. That evening, along with the entire transport, I entered the camp through a huge gate on which you could see a sign in iron letters reading: "Arbeit macht frei."* Immediately after entering we were chased into the baths, to the sauna. At that time I was not aware that this infamous phrase evoked feelings of terror in all the prisoners. That gate was the entrance to the valley of death. It was impossible for anyone to imagine what awaited a human being in this death trap. We were ushered through a place that looked like an amphitheatre and from there into the showers. We undressed completely and sat down on the benches. Since the room was unheated we shivered from cold. We waited for the SS men to visit us. They arrived. "Achtung!" the *blokowa* shouted. We jumped up from our places and stood naked in front of a large group of SS men who looked us over slowly, with disdain in their eyes.

*"Work makes you free."

It was terrible. Old women with large stomachs and sagging breasts, poor and wrinkled, stood at attention in front of them, taking pains at all costs to hide their age.

"Where is the barber?" shouted an SS man.

Barber? What kind of barber? What kind of a ball are we going to, naked with a fancy hairdo? A few prisoners hustled into the room, with large scissors in their hands. They situated themselves in front of the stairs.

"Why are you staring, you idiots? Form a line and step up to have your hair cut." The *blokowa* was shouting and hitting people in the face, pushing them toward the barber. She hit hard, apparently wanting to demonstrate to the SS men how well qualified she was for the job.

The shearing of the sheep had started, and with scissors so dull that they tore bunches of hair out of our heads. There was one big difference between us and sheep, however. The sheep bleated as they were being shorn, but we stood there in silence with tears streaming down our cheeks.

"Spread your legs," yelled the *blokowa*. And the body hair was shorn too.

All of this took place very quickly, to the accompaniment of shouts and blows, which fell thickly on our heads and shoulders. We ceased to exist as thinking, feeling entities. We were not allowed any modesty in front of these strange men. We were nothing more than objects on which they performed their duties, nonsentient things that they could examine from all angles. It did not bother them that cutting hair close to the skin with dull scissors was excruciatingly painful. It did not bother them that we were women and that without our hair we felt totally humiliated.

Once again, we were sitting on the benches, naked, the hair on our heads, what was left of it, cut in layers, all of us hunched over from the cold. I was looking for acquaintances among those transformed figures, and truly, I did not recognize anybody. How tragic, and at the same time, how comic, everybody looked. Think of it. Once upon a time, each of us was capable of awakening feelings of love and affection. Each of us once had some value, her own world of intimate dreams and desires.

In a few hours we were robbed of everything that had been ours personally. We were shown that here in Auschwitz we were just numbers, without faces or souls.

"Which one is Liza? Step out," shouted the *blokowa*.

Liza was a young, pretty girl. I remember how, in Bialystok, she used to arrange musical evenings, at which she sang Russian songs and arias from operas and operettas.

"You know how to sing?" the *blokowa* asked, and without waiting for an answer she told her to sing something in German for the SS men. Naked, with her head shorn, Liza started singing in a deep voice, "Auch ich war einst ein reicher."* In front of her lounged the SS men and the barbers, with scissors in their hands. The *blokowa* and all of us in the auditorium watched that scene and were witnesses to it.

I was so tired that I began to feel faint. The air undulated in front of me, and everything—the SS men, Liza, and the men with the scissors—started revolving around me. Nothing was real. It was as if I were looking at a picture from another world. Suddenly the SS man who was standing closest to Liza hit her with a stick and told her to shut up. In a minute we were pushed into another room, the shower room. We stood in front of the showers, waiting for the warm water. Suddenly we jumped as if we had been scalded. Ice water came spurting out of the showers. "Wash!" bellowed the *blokowa* when we jumped away from the freezing water. Our teeth chattered from the cold, and the cold water came pouring down on us as if we were standing under a waterfall.

In the next room we were given any old rags that were handy. I was given a long, black, silk dress, full of holes, and nothing else besides that. Outside there was a very hard frost. For our feet they gave us wooden clogs and no stockings. I looked like a typical *zugang* with a shaved head, in a silk dress full of holes, with no boots, and with fear and hunger in my eyes. I imagined that thousands of fingers were pointing at me saying, "Here is a victim you can hit; you can pour your anger out on her and she will not protest, not even if you perform unusual acts of torture on her. If

*"Once I used to be rich also."

she can't take it, that will be even better. There will be one *zugang* less."

We were taken to the block of *zugangi*. It consisted of a huge barracks, with a long brick oven, about fifty centimeters high, running the whole length of it. On both sides of the barracks were deep trenches. The sleeping accommodations were in the trenches and on two decks of shelves built into the walls. There were some soiled blankets, and that was it. I pushed myself into one of the spaces and tried to sleep. But that was impossible. All night long the women scrambled from their sleeping places and went outside, where, in front of the block, stood a wooden chest at which you could take care of your personal needs. The women had colds, and they would barely have returned to their lodgings before they had to jump out again. The bustle in the barracks was constant. Every few minutes the gate creaked.

"What's going on here? What kind of promenades do we have here?" shouted one of the functionaries who slept in the room. She rushed out of the block and found a few women with stretched-out behinds over the chest. I heard moaning. None of us would allow herself to scream. All the women standing over the chest were pushed into it. Then the functionary proclaimed, "Nobody had better move, because if you do I will kill you like a dog." Everything was quiet. Only low sighing and moaning. Suddenly I noticed an old lady in the next bed squat and start peeing in a pot from which she would drink coffee in the morning. She looked at me, embarrassed, and put her finger to her lips so that I would not say anything to anybody. I assured her with a nod of my head. Could she do otherwise?

By now I had been on the block of the Jewish *zugangi* for a whole week. During this entire period I doubt that I had managed to get even as much as two bowls of soup for lunch. As soon as I would get close to the soup can I would be pushed away brutally. Those who were stronger took my portion. When I tried to object I was hit over the head with my own bowl. In the block with me was a young beautiful girl from Bialystok named Karola. Every crumb of bread that she could get hold of, and every spoonful of soup she could grab she shared with me. If not for her I doubt whether I would have survived the hard lot of a *zugang*.

January 1944 was unusually cold. The stars were still glittering in the frosty sky when they chased us out to the front of the block for roll call. As the cliché would have it, "the stars winked at us happily." I trembled from cold in my long, black silk dress dotted with holes. To me the stars looked vengeful and pitiless. They lined us up in ranks of five. Every row had to be straight and was formed according to height, from tallest to shortest. The poor old women did not understand what those crazed *blokowe* required of them. Without scruple, young, well-dressed, well-fed women beat the faces of women old enough to be their mothers. Standing in front of the ranks of taut women, the *sztubowa* shouted, "Achtung!" which brought out the *blokowa*. She was a young, Jewish girl from Slovakia, about twenty years of age, beautiful, elegant, and slightly pink from sleep and frost. She was beautifully dressed. I remember that she had on a blue rain cape with a hood which was tossed over her winter coat. It seemed to me at the time that she was unusually beautiful, almost an unearthly being. She floated through the rows of taut bodies with dignity. Apparently she liked the way we stood, because she stood aside without saying a word. We had to wait a long time for the SS men to appear so that we could have a proper roll call that would ascertain that not even one prisoner might be hiding and that all the prisoners were standing there ready to welcome the angel of death.

I sat on my bunk gazing at the scene that was being played out in front of me. From the moment I got to Auschwitz I was completely detached. I disconnected my heart and intellect in an act of self-defense, despair, and hopelessness. I sipped hot coffee, which I had managed to procure, looking at the unreal world around me. A few beds away from me there were two Greek women asleep. They were very dark and beautiful. The short one, a cheerful, helpful woman, had already managed to get to the top of the block of *zugangen*. She was a dressmaker who had somehow beguiled the *blokowa* with her skill and then spent her whole day sitting in the *blokowa's* room sewing. At night she would return to the barracks well fed and brimming with confidence. A young girl of about fifteen slept next to her. She was skinny and had huge eyes. All day she sat on her bed, her knees under her chin, and cried. Tears big as peas ran down her cheeks. She would not win the fight for life. She would perish for sure. Cruelty would squash her; she would not be able to resist it. She was not physically strong, and had no experience, no meanness, no selfishness.

With some difficulty we managed to communicate. She knew a little German. "Mother, my mother," she whispered in despair, "went to the gas as soon as we got to the camp. She is not here any more. Only her ashes remain." In the evening she quietly sang a Hungarian song for me, a song about a mother which became very popular after the war. She sang in such a way that until this very day I remember her and her song. She missed maternal warmth in this terrible world that was entirely beyond her comprehension.

The Jewish women from Holland were big, broad, and tall, with light, freckled complexions. In their eyes you could see only wonder, not even fear or despair, only bewilderment. They were amazed when they received heavy blows from the *sztubowe* and from the other low-life characters who had quickly acquired the camp life style: hit if you do not want to be beaten. They did not push in line for soup or bread, and they slept on the floor because a more aggressive person had taken the upper bunk. They did not even bother to wash their faces.

"Where can we wash in this dump?" one of them countered in

amazement when I asked her why she did not wash. "There is no bathtub here," she explained.

It was important to wash, even if it meant rubbing your face with a fistful of snow. The effort to wash your face is an expression of life. The women from Holland did not fight to survive. They very quickly became "mussulmen," and many of them died right on the block of the *zugangen*.

The Jewish women from Germany behaved in such a way as to keep themselves separated from the rest of the prisoners. "How did we get here with this rabble from the East?" said their offended expressions. "After all, we are from Germany." Their heads were shaven, just like ours, and they were dressed like clowns, the same as we were, but they still imagined that the Germans would eventually remove them from the Jewish block and that the theory of *herrenvolk* would serve to elevate them above the Jews from other countries. "I am German, not Jewish," one of them, an older woman, kept repeating. "What will the SS men do with us? They can't treat us like this." These women despised us, their fellow victims, more than they hated the SS men who had taken their homes and pushed them to the edge of the abyss. "I am German," the old woman yelled at the *sztubowa* as the *sztubowa* pushed her away from the soup can.

"As far as I'm concerned, you're a stinking *zugang*, just like everybody else around here," the *sztubowa* shouted back at her as she delivered a blow to her face.

Where does this pride come from? Where do they get that self-assurance? It was the Germans who started this present persecution of Jews, and the trouble started in Germany much earlier than in other countries. I remember Jewish refugees from Hitler's Germany who came to Poland in 1934. They knew by that time what the Germans are capable of. They had witnessed for themselves the terrible methods that the Germans were ready to use to destroy the Jews. Why, therefore, did they look at us with such disgust in this death camp? They probably subscribed to the German theory, "Germany above everything." So how was it possible that their fellow Germans should force them to mingle shoulder-to-shoulder with this East European rabble?

The blocks of the Jewish *zugangen*, like all the other blocks, were ruled by the Jewish women from Slovakia. In 1944 they were the real aristocrats of the camp. It seems strange, but in this congregation of misery, baseness, and fear, they sparkled with an unusual luster. They were the first prisoners in Auschwitz, and they felt a certain pride in having built the camp. When they were brought there in 1940, there was nothing but swampland, but now there were barracks, blocks, offices, and streets.

"While we were building this place," they said, "and were being plagued by malaria, you were sleeping in warm beds." They spoke with such hatred and contempt to the *zugangen* as if the *zugangen* deserved nothing better than ill treatment and death. We existed only so they might have somebody to kick around, somebody to beat up on, somebody to serve as a background to their reflected glory.

To the right of the block entrance was a room where the *blokowa* and the clerk lived. Sometimes, when the door was partly open, I could manage to peek in. There were two beds of normal width. On the beds were two pink silk quilts. The room also contained a table, chairs, glasses, and dishes. Sometimes the *blokowa* and the clerk would come into the block early in the morning wearing long silk bathrobes. I thought I must be dreaming. They received all these wonders from their fellow countrywomen who worked in the *effektenkammer*, where they sorted out the things brought into the camp by the *zugangen*. In exchange for these items they gave the workers from the *effektenkammer* bread, margarine, and salami, which they stole out of our rations. The SS men saw the splendor in which the camp functionaries lived, but all this took place with their silent approval. It was a devilish system in which the SS men and the functionaries were united by a chain of cruelty. The contrast between their splendor and our misery kept them constantly aware of what they stood to lose in the event that they failed to carry out the orders of the SS men. They used whatever methods were necessary to assure their own survival and their relatively comfortable way of life. If the voice of conscience chanced to awake in them, they would quiet it continuously with the same arguments: "We suffered so much the first few years. We lived through those hard times. Now we are not going to die for the sake of some dirty *zugang*."

The *sztubowe*, of whom there were a few, slept comfortably in the block, often on goose down. Among them were Polish Jews from the earlier transports. They were the leaders on the block, and in most instances they were vulgar and coarse. They tried with all their might to ingratiate themselves with the *blokowa* and the *kapo*. They marched with a mannish step, their arms swinging at their sides. Every few minutes they would dole out some fire and brimstone from which it was impossible to escape without humiliating yourself. The women used to walk around with blackened eyes, which we elegantly called sunglasses. Cruelty towards the weak and humility towards the strong was the rule here.

We used to sit on our beds, silent, hunched over, waiting for the worst. In her long robe the *blokowa* would inspect the block, looking straight in front of her. She did not see us at all. She walked with a slow, majestic step, her proud head held high. You would not believe that she was a prisoner, just like the rest of us, and the lowest category of prisoner, at that, a Jew. Once she caught an old woman in front of the block who was apparently unable to reach the toilet, which was a considerable distance from the block. We heard an especially inhuman moaning of a victim being beaten without pity: "Oh you swine! Do you think I'm going to suffer for you? Die, you stinker," she finished. In front of the block lay a rag of a human being, covered with mud. Madame *blokowa* returned to her warm room.

DEATH OF THE *ZUGANG*

After that first week on the block of the *zugangen* I felt myself reaching the limits of my endurance. I knew that I would not be able to manage. I would simply be crushed by those who were stronger than I. I was hungry. All around me raged an animalistic struggle for existence, a battle for a little bit of watery soup, even for a little bit of water. I was cold during the day and cold at night. I hatched all sorts of plots in my sick head. I wanted to do something that would attract the attention of some noble soul who must have existed there, though I could not imagine how. I could not decide what I should do, and I did not find that noble soul. I was dying, perishing in this terrible world.

Then I decided to commit suicide. Truly, there was no other way out. This may appear strange, but what bothered me most in my desperate situation were the naked decaying corpses lying in front of the block. Every morning the *sztubowa* pulled dead women out of the beds. She immediately stripped them naked, dragged them through the whole block, and heaved them into the mud. As she dragged them through the block by one hand you could hear the bones crack, and the loosely hanging heads banged on the cement. I thought in despair that these might have been highly intelligent, talented beings—actresses, painters, poets. Or maybe they were just women who loved and who were loved in return. Maybe they had children to whom they were most beautiful. Maybe they were dreamers. Maybe they believed in miracles that would redeem them from this Hell. But no miracle had occurred, and now they were being dragged through the mud without honor and without pity.

I was frightened by the thought that tomorrow they would be dragging me through the block, a nameless dishonored corpse, unmourned by anyone. Although I did not believe in life after death, still I trembled at the thought of what was going to happen to me after I died.

I decided that on the coming Thursday I would make an end of it. I twined a shirt into a rope, which I intended to slip around my neck after everyone was asleep. After roll call, half frozen, I curled up on the upper bunk and listened to the women around me gossiping. I was listening, but I heard nothing. Having made my decision I felt serene. The young Greek girl, sad as always, was sitting next to me. She scratched herself nervously, tormented by a rash.

"If the Germans were to see the rash they would send me to the gas right away," she whispered with fear. "If you could give me some ointment I would smear it on, and in a couple of days I would be healthy."

Sorry. I had no ointment. I answered her request politely, but my thoughts were far away from the world that surrounded me. I was thinking about my own death, feeling its cold breath washing over me. High on the ceiling burned a small lamp; the whole block was submerged in half darkness.

Suddenly a familiar voice broke through the wall of consciousness. Someone was standing at my bed, someone familiar and close. Who could it be? I bent over, violently, and saw Sonia Rozawska. At the sight of me, Sonia became quiet. I did not have to say anything. She saw my strength ebbing. The entire nervous strain of the last few weeks rose to the surface at this moment. I sank into unconsciousness.

From 1938 to 1939 Sonia and I both had been prisoners in the Fordonia prison. We had been political prisoners. Later on, when the Russians controlled Bialystok, we both taught in the Bialystok school. In August 1941 we found ourselves prisoners again, this time in the Bialystok Ghetto. At that time we both joined the Jewish anti-Hitler volunteer army. In February 1943, during the first *aktzia*, the Germans took Sonia. It seems that she was sent directly to Auschwitz. She had been here for a year by this time. She knew the camp and the people, and she had become adept at living in this Hell.

Sonia had hair, warm clothes, and boots. By our standards she looked well fed.

"Don't torment yourself," Sonia whispered in my ear. "We will have you out of here by tomorrow. We will 'organize' a warm sweater and boots for you. I will bring food for you. Do you know why I came here? To find friends and help them as much as we can. There are many of our people in the camp—meaning the international anti-Hitler organization. We are not without our means, even in this Hell."

She ran quickly, because she lived quite a distance from our block, but she returned after a short interval. She brought a sweater, boots, and some bread. Now the *sztubowa* took notice of me; she asked me if I wanted to sleep next to her. Now I was somebody. I had protectors. Now it was not a bad idea to stay on good terms with me.

"Did you get your supper?" the *sztubowa* asked.

God! How base everything was. Sonia left after a short while because she had to get back before they closed the gate.

"Things will be different tomorrow," Sonia told me before she left. "Just keep calm. You have a lot of acquaintances whom you'll see tomorrow."

I hid the noose that was waiting to deliver me under the mattress, and I fell asleep with hope in my heart. I felt so good that I began to thaw from inner warmth.

"Things will be different tomorrow." Those were prophetic words though Sonia did not imagine how things would be different. Right after roll call the block was closed. No one was permitted to leave. "*Blocksperre*"—so it was called in camp language. The *blokowa* stood guard at the gate so that nobody could slip away. The *sztubowe* chased us from the beds and started to line us up in pairs.

"Selection!" The word passed from mouth to mouth. They will look us over, examine us carefully from all angles; some will be chosen to live and others to die. "Selection!" We repeat that terrible word. No one was yelling; no one was crying; no one was trying to defend herself. What was keeping us back? Was it the fear of that kind of death that could be terrible? Perhaps the icy breath of death takes away a human being's ability to act. Maybe one simply does not want to fight, just to live among the people who created this kind of a world.

I knew that for me selection meant death. Nevertheless, I was serene. I observed objectively everything that was happening around me. Even the yelling of the *sztubowe*, who were doing their best to make sure that we would take our last walk in an orderly fashion, came to me as if from a distance.

Finally, we were taken to the baths. We walked into a tremendous circle made by all the *sztubowe* holding each other by the hand, making sure that none of us would slip out of the circle. Later the *blokowe* kept counting and re-counting us for a long time, and no matter how they counted there was always one number missing. Two of the *sztubowe* tore off in the direction of the block, and a minute later they returned leading an eighty-year-old woman who had no idea what was happening around her. They laughed with pleasure at having found their lost sheep so quickly, and they were satisfied that everything was proceeding so smoothly. Without a shade of sadness or scruple they were dragging this defenseless old lady by the arms, her head hanging down as if she were a manikin, leading her to certain death.

The first few pairs went to the baths. Right at the entrance you had to undress completely. Then you had to walk past the table where the commandant of the camp and the camp doctors sat, with the blood sucker Mengele at the head. The condemned person's number was recorded, and then, after the inspection, the condemned person had to take a different door leading to the other side of the bath. There nobody guarded them. The doorlatch fell.

Anxiety grew among the women as they watched the procession going to the bath. Some tried to run away, to slip through the circle of hands that surrounded them. The *blokowe* yelled and beat them mercilessly. I stood in line, waiting my turn. What was happening around me was so terrible that I could not make myself believe it was real. At one point I noticed that the little Greek girl hid behind an old chest that was standing not too far away. She did not want to die, but she knew that if the German doctors saw the scabs on her body they would send her to the gas, even though her rash could be cured in a few days. I did not look in her direction, though I knew that they would find her and push her into the bath. They did find her. They dragged the beautiful little girl out of her hiding place and pushed her into the bath. Not long after, I looked up to the second floor. A window opened and the little Greek girl jumped out, a rag thrown across her naked body. She fell, then got up and quickly started to run away, but the *sztubowe* descended on her. They beat her, at the same time screaming: "What do you think, you stinker? You think that I'm going to go to the gas for you?" They dragged her into the bath for the last judgment.

SALVATION

Suddenly a young girl appeared in front of me. Dressed in a sports coat, with a hood on her head, she went down the line asking, in a hushed voice, "Who is a friend of Sonia?" I became proud. Could they mean me? "That's me," I said, not completely sure that they really meant me.

She looked at me quickly, as though she could read me completely with this one look. That is how people looked at each other in Auschwitz, as though they undressed each other with a glance. "Come with me," she whispered. "How can I?" I replied. "The *sztubowe*." I was afraid of their blows. "Don't ask," she said. "Just come." I stepped out of the line. The hands of the *sztubowe* parted before my guide. We stepped outside the chain that surrounded the people condemned to death. Eva (that was the stranger's name) led me along a narrow path. She took me to the rear of the bath house, where those who had lived through the selection were waiting. I was saved.

We stood there for a long time, shifting from leg to leg, oppressed by cold and fatigue. We waited for the rest of those who were not going to the gas this time. When the selection was finished, we returned to the block. Without a word we lay down on the beds, unable to exert any effort. The *sztubowe* also sat motionless, dejected and silent. Even those who were familiar with death and with the crimes of Auschwitz saw in the selections the uncertainty of their own existence.

The first day after the selection our block looked terrible. Everyone returned, even those whose number had been written down in the book of death. They had a few days respite from the gas. The little Greek girl was lying on her bunk, injured from her desperate jump through the window. She was inscribed for the gas. Because of some scabs a young beautiful girl would be cut off from life. I did not talk to her, though she lay no more than an arm's length from me. I was ashamed that I was to live.

There were some other people from Bialystok on the block with me: Sojkow and her two daughters. Mrs. Sojkow was written down for the gas. She was an older woman but full of vigor and initiative. Before the war she had been a small-town merchant. She had been affluent and believed in the might of gold. I remember that in the Bialystok prison she was able to procure bread and ham for her family, her daughters and grandchildren. With the gold that she managed to bring into the cell she was able to bribe the guard to bring her the provisions she needed. But the gold did not help her save her grandchildren: Niunke, a clever eight-year-old, and her two brothers. All of them had been sent to the gas by the Germans. And now Mrs. Sojkow herself was condemned to the gas. Although she was still alive, her two daughters cried over her death. The three of them sat in a tight embrace, crying, and from time to time the mother would interrupt the crying to give them a bit of advice.

Suddenly I saw Sojkow get up and move to my side. It was really hard for me to look at her, her nose sharpened and her mouth tightened with grief. A condemned person, but condemned for what crime? Why did she have to perish like a strangled rat? At this minute I thought it would be more merciful if they were to take them to the gas immediately. Why this waiting for death? Maybe because waiting for death would be even worse than death itself. The old lady sat next to me, a living corpse.

"I don't know when they will take me," she started sheepishly. "Please excuse me for any wrong I may have done to you." In the Bialystok Ghetto we had lived in one room, and yet we never fought. What sins could have been committed against me by this unfortunate lady whom the Nazis would not allow to die a natural death? I reminded myself of a similar scene in Bialystok when the Gestapo lined us all up against the wall with our hands on our necks. We were sure that this was death. At that time, also, Mrs. Sojkow called to the rest of us to forgive her any wrongs she might have committed against us unintentionally. Mrs. Sojkow believed in the world after death, and she wanted to go to heaven unencumbered by sin. What could I tell her? To comfort her by telling her that I thought she had a chance of evading death would have been dishonest, and to talk to her as if she were already a corpse would have been inhuman. For the first time I shed bitter tears.

The subdued murmuring coming from all corners of the block was suddenly interrupted by a desperate yell: "Why was my number written down?" cried Hela from an upper bunk. She was a young and very handsome woman. In the Bialystok Ghetto Mrs. Hela had run a small store out of her apartment. For a few pennies you could buy a piece of bread. In the Bialystok prison they took her four-year-old daughter, and now she was assigned to the gas. "Let the *blokowa* come here and let her accompany me to the SS men," Mrs. Hela pleaded. The *sztubowe* moved in her direction, but with some quick movements she took off her clothes and stood naked in the upper bunk. "Look at me. How could they write down my number?" She spun around, showing her body from all angles, and particularly exhibiting her breasts.

"She is really young and pretty. Why did they write her number down?" I trembled at that terrible logic, as though there were some justification in killing the sick, the elderly, and the unattractive. I looked at the old faces, the bowed heads, and I felt sorry for them. I tried not to think about my own salvation though Eva's form shimmered before my eyes. I tried to dampen the joy that wanted to surge through me because this time I had eluded the angel of death. Who was this Eva before whom the ring that was so tightly closed for everyone else had opened? Why did she come looking for me? Sonia probably asked her to come because Sonia was unable to come herself. She had led me to the other side of the bath, endangering her own life. Why did she do it? The whole time she had walked briskly in front of me, not looking around. From time to time she had said, as if to herself, "Don't look around. Just walk behind me the whole way." When we finally had arrived in a safe place, behind the bath, she had disappeared.

They brought lunch, but nobody ate. The fights that usually took place at the soup can did not occur. The *sztubowa* called a few of the prisoners to come get the soup but no one stirred from her place. The cans were returned to the kitchen full. You do not take your own death lightly. It is impossible to live in a world where there is no room for joy. Poor *zugang*. More than half of our block were condemned to death. When will they take them? How long will they have to wait before the death sentence is implemented?

I was so engrossed in my thoughts that for a long time the fact that someone was calling my name did not register. "Sara Nomberg," somebody was shouting in a very loud voice. It was Masza Zyskinol. I looked at her and thought that I must be dreaming. Where had she come from? Masza was originally from Lublin. We had attended the same school, and Masza had matriculated a few years before I had. Then she had gone to France to study. She used to come back to Lublin for the summer, and it was during those summers that we became close friends. Masza was a Communist, a slightly rebellious Communist, as she described herself, since she did not always agree with the party line. On our long walks through the parks of Lublin we used to discuss the problems of the world. When I was released from prison in 1934 I returned to Lublin, where I was told that Masza was in Paris. How did she get to Auschwitz?

She descended on me breathlessly. "Tell me, were you in the bath? Did they look you over? Did they write down your number?" The words came tumbling in one breath. "You weren't, so everything is alright. You look terrible. I guess you're not used to it. In a few days we'll get you out of here." Where to, nobody said. At this point I did not care. Even the encounter with a dear friend did not make any impression on me. In my thoughts I was far away from her.

THE ROAR OF THE BEAST

I ran into Eva the day after the selection. I was very surprised that she would want to come to the *zugangen* block, where grief reigned among those of us who were still alive. Since she was a clerk in the neighboring block, she belonged to the elite of the camp. That is why the chain of hands opened before her during the selection. Thanks to her position, she was allowed to move freely in the vicinity of the bath house.

I looked at that sweet, likable young face, which to me appeared to be almost not of this earth. Auschwitz predisposed you to mystical comparisons. To me she was an angel who had snatched me from a terrible death. I just stood there speechless, listening to what she was telling me about herself. She had been brought to Auschwitz in 1942 in a transport of Jews from Radom. She was sixteen years old at the time. Her parents, who had come with her, were sent to the gas immediately. She was left alone on the block of the *zugangen*. Her parents had been teachers of German in the local *gimnasium*, and as a result she spoke German fluently. The *blokowa*, who took notice of her, recommended her to the secretariat as a *läufer*. A *läufer* was not a simple courier. The area of the camp extended for several kilometers, and the camp was divided into many areas separated by gates. All of the administrative reports and orders were carried from the main administrative office to the blocks by the *lauferki*. Usually they were young, beautiful girls, uniformly dressed in sports outfits with white collars, and with the word *"lauferka"* on the sleeve. As carriers of both good and bad news, they were able to move through the camp freely and were treated respectfully. The camp underground tried to enlist these girls in the organization because they were an excellent source of information on what the Germans were planning to do in the camp. The *lauferki* could also serve as a communications link among various groups in the organization without being noticed. Thanks to the *lauferki* it was possible to shelter comrades who were ailing because one of the *läufer*'s duties was to lead prisoners to their assigned *komandos*.

At first Eva knew nothing about the existence of a resistance movement in the camp, so, like Mercury, she carried the messages of the gods to the *blokowe*. She had it made. She lived in a separate room and had plenty of food. In an instant she had been elevated to a place among the camp elite.

One July day, as she was performing her usual chores, carrying a report to the camp Gestapo, she saw a friend from Radom; he was badly beaten and covered with blood. He was surprised to see her but quickly lowered his eyes, not letting on that he knew her. But in that instant when their eyes met, she recognized his look of contempt. He despised her for having sold herself to the Germans. The Gestapo was torturing the young man, trying to force him to inform on his comrades in the resistance. Every morning when she came to the Gestapo she saw the young boy, and every day she saw the contempt in his look and the pain in his body.

"I wanted to help him," Eva told me, "but I didn't know how. I started looking for people who could give me advice. I knew nothing about the resistance, but I had already made the acquaintance of many important women, and I decided to talk to them. First of all, I wanted them to tell me whether I should give up my job as a *läufer*. The contempt in the young man's look gave me no peace. As it turned out, the resistance was also trying to make contact with me. I kept my job as a *läufer*, carrying messages for my friends. A few weeks after I had started carrying messages for the resistance, my friend was shot. We couldn't help him. I kept my job as a *läufer* for a whole year, but finally I got fed up with it. I felt that if I were to stay among the Germans any longer I would wind up doing something foolish. Now I am just a clerk on the block. The *blokowa* is a Jew from Slovakia, a coarse woman. But I still have some clout among the *sztubowe* because of my previous job. That's why I was able to lead you around the bath house. The morning of the selection Sonia sent me a message to meet her at the gate, because she had something very important to tell me. During selection the gates dividing one field from another are closed. Sonia is on field 'B' and we are on field 'A.' I met Sonia at the gate and she told me to find you and keep you from going to the selection. I succeeded, and I am very pleased that I did."

For me Eva has always remained a being not of this world. Even after the war, when she found me and came to Lublin to see me, I could not free myself of that first impression. I always envisioned her as she looked that day when she led me through the narrow path to the back of the bath house.

Three days after the selection the *oberkapo*, Bubi, came into our block. That was the first time I saw her. All of the women in Auschwitz were afraid of her. She wore men's clothing: pants and a sweater. Her hair was cut short. She had a deep voice and quick, nervous movements. Next to her number she wore a black triangle, which indicated that she was a criminal prisoner. Bubi was *oberkapo* of field "A," and she ruled with an iron fist. Early in the morning she came to pick her victims whose names had been written down on a list. With her came the *blokowa* of Block 25, known as the block of death. The women condemned to the gas were interned there until there were enough of them so that it would "pay" to run the gas. This *blokowa* of the death block was called the "Beautiful Cyla." She was about eighteen years old, the youngest of the Slovak Jews, and looked like an angel. But every prisoner feared her.

We all crouched in our bunks, frightened, helpless in the face of the mass murder that was to take place before our very eyes. No one cried out, nobody wept. When they entered our block a deathly silence descended over all: Bubi in her high boots, whip in hand; Cyla, the *blokowa*; and all the *sztubowe*. The gate that led into the block was locked. A table at which the clerk and the *blokowa* sat was set in the middle of the block. Bubi and Cyla stood off to the side. "Achtung," barked the *blokowa*. We jumped out of our bunks and stood at attention. Bubi surveyed the entire block with a slow eye. She looked everyone over carefully.

"Now," said the *blokowa* in German, "you will form a line and pull up your left sleeve so that your number shows. Slowly, one by one, you will walk around the table and show your number."

Without a word of protest we lined up and moved in the direction of the table. Today, as I think of it all, I understand the questions sometimes put to me: "Why did the Jews go so quietly? Why did they let themselves be taken to the gas chambers without protest?" There were about five hundred women on the block whose numbers appeared on the death list. Why didn't they pounce on Bubi, Cyla, the *blokowa*, and the rest of the attendants to send their tormentors to death before they themselves died? What did they have to lose? In Auschwitz I was witness to many such quiet expeditions to the gas chambers. At the time I always asked those painful questions of myself: Why are they silent? Why don't they cry out? We had already discussed this in Auschwitz, and for those of us who went through that Hell, the affair was completely clear. When the Jews marched off to the gas after they had arrived at Auschwitz, they simply did not know where they were going, and when we told them they did not believe us.

In the summer of 1944, when massive transports of Jews arrived from all over Europe, they went straight to the gas chambers. The resistance delegated a comrade to the *komando* working on the ramp who took packages from the arriving Jews. A young, energetic Austrian was assigned to work there; he was to tell the unsuspecting victims where they were headed. They absolutely refused to believe him. Some of them went to the SS men who were stationed at the unloading of the wagons and asked: "Is it true that we are going to the showers to be gassed?"

That is how it was with new arrivals who still felt like human beings with human rights. Those who had already gone through a few weeks of school in beatings, hunger, maltreatment, and the loss of feeling and humanity were incapable of resisting. A wild beast, before pouncing on his victim, will roar so piercingly that the victim will become paralyzed with fright and will be incapable of running away. The victim just crouches and waits for the end. That is how it was with the five hundred women on the death list. After a few weeks on the block of the *zugangen*, the daily round of abuse, tattered clothes, of being treated as if we were rags, not women, then the selections—all of that was the roar that robbed us of any human reaction to the injustice of death. We stood in line, hunched over, waiting for the beast to tear us apart.

The impetus for every human act is survival. No matter how miniscule it may be, in the mind of every human being this faint hope grows into a command: Try, and perhaps you will succeed.

In the camp, when your number was already inscribed in the book of death and there was no longer the slightest possibility of survival, the will was paralyzed.

Bubi called out the numbers that appeared before her, and the clerk checked to make sure the number was not on the list. Those whose numbers were on the list were ordered to stand on the side near Cyla. A young woman, not very tall, tried to hide among the bunks. She hid like a hare running from the hounds. The *sztubowe* pounced on her. Bubi measured out a few blows to her head, and from that point on everything proceeded in perfect order.

Madam Hela did not give up the idea of persuading the judges who sat at the table that her number had gotten onto the list by mistake, that she was young, healthy, and beautiful. When she got close to the table she quickly undressed and stood naked in front of Bubi. She kneeled in front of her and begged for mercy. I turned to stone. I felt that something terrible was going to happen. Bubi did not hit her. She just looked at her for a long time without saying anything. Finally, she told her to stand aside. She would not even let her get dressed.

Order was interrupted just once more. A young girl whose mother was assigned to the gas did not want to be separated from her. She wanted to die with her mother. They tore her from her mother by force.

When the congregation was complete, Cyla lined the women up in ranks of five. Then Bubi put the naked, beautiful Hela at the head of the column. They walked out into the frost and the snow with Hela in the lead.

Just think of it. So many women were sent to their deaths without the help of one SS man. The Germans managed to do their dirty work with the hands of the prisoners.

had been in the infirmary for three days. The day after "the chosen" were taken off to the death block, the *schreiberka* came to see me. She told me to get ready, that she would take me to the infirmary, and that I would be admitted as a hospital patient. "I am not sick," I protested. I was terribly afraid of the hospital. During the selection I had seen what was done to the sick and the weak in Auschwitz.

"I am not asking you whether you want to or not," she answered. "I have an order from Orli, the *lageralteste* of the area. So don't talk, just get ready."

When Masha was here she mentioned to me that Orli was a German Communist. Since Hitler had come to power in 1933 she had been in concentration camps. Now, in Auschwitz, she was administrator of the whole area. She had a great deal of power and could use it to help comrades. If Orli told them to bring me, nothing bad would happen to me. Maybe this was the help from my friends that I had been waiting for.

Right after breakfast, which I now received regularly, I went to the clinic along with the sick women who had been chosen by the *sztubowe* from among those who had been groaning with pain. The area was adjacent to field "A." All we had to do to get there was to go through the gate. The area was no different from the rest of the camp: the same barracks and the same barren surroundings without a single tree. Nothing but barracks and dirt and trampled snow. The first barracks on the corner was the infirmary. Many women who had been brought from the other blocks were already waiting here. In the area there were blocks and infirmaries, both Aryan and Jewish. I was taken to a Jewish infirmary. We waited outside, frozen and hunched over with the cold. Although they were terribly frightened, these women had decided to report sick. They could barely stand on their feet. Many of them were suffering from dysentery. It was a common camp sickness. The body could not hold a crumb of food and grew progressively weaker. These women were horribly emaciated, with green faces, giving off rank odors. Some of the women had excruciatingly painful sores on their breasts, but they did not want to stay in the hospital and only asked to have the sores dressed. They were afraid of the selections that took place frequently on the Jewish blocks.

After we had waited for a few minutes, the clerk took us into the infirmary. Along the walls were closets stocked with bandages. There was a large table on which the sick were examined and where wounds were dressed. A smaller table stood in the middle of the room. On it was a file of registration cards. Behind the table sat a young girl who was apparently a clerk. We stood in line. The entering patients went up to the clerk and gave her their names and numbers. The clerk searched for the name in the box that was in front of her. If she did not find it, she made out a sick card. With this card you went to the table where the doctors and nurses were at work.

I stood in line next to women who could hardly stand on their feet. I received a card and went to the doctor, though I did not know what to tell her. The doctor was small, young, and unusually beautiful. She was a Czech Jew. Before I could get close to her, she nodded in my direction to calm me down. As I waited my turn in this cold, terrible, brutal world, my heart was singing a happy song about brotherhood and friendship.

Marusia—that was the nurse's name—was also Czech. When she saw my card, she gave me a warm look, and a sunny smile lit up her face. "Nazdar" ("Good luck"), she whispered softly. She shoved me aside and told me to wait patiently.

Marusia dressed the oozing, pussy sores skillfully. She lanced abscesses that formed under the arms. Everything took place in silence, without anaesthesia and without groans. The only arguments that took place occurred when it was recommended that a patient go to the hospital. The old prisoners, who knew what it meant, did not want to go to the hospital. The new ones asked to stay in the area "because they were too sick to work." These women had to be advised that it was a mistake to remain here, and when that did not help, they had to be chased with a shout. After everyone had been examined at the infirmary, about twenty of the most seriously ill were directed to different hospital blocks. The *schreiberka* lined them up in pairs. Then she took the sick cards on which the diagnoses were recorded, as well as the block numbers to which the patients were assigned. I was the only one left in the infirmary.

Now both of them greeted me—Marusia, the nurse, and Mancy, the doctor. "We are Czech Communists. We know all about you. You will work with us in the infirmary as a clerk. Unfortunately, there is no vacancy right now, so we are admitting you as a patient on the hospital block. You will only sleep on the block. Early in the morning, before roll call, you will come here to us and will work with us." Marusia spoke very fast and with a smile. It was obvious that she was trying to convince herself that the matter was well taken care of, and that everything would come out well. Mancy was quiet. "You know, a lot of our friends work in this area and on the blocks. Masha probably will come soon, and she will explain everything."

The area was seeded with members of the anti-Fascist organizations. Many of the *blokowe*, *schreiberki*, doctors, and nurses were our friends. This had been accomplished by Orli, director of the whole area. She had a decisive voice in the appointment of functionaries and had to make appointments within reason. She could not remove those who had squeezed into the area via other channels. In this area, the functionaries were safer than they were anywhere else in the camp.

Officially, I was supposed to be sick. According to my sick card I belonged in the hospital, but in actuality I was supposed to work in the infirmary. Mancy tried to ease my anxieties by telling me that there are many functionaries on the block who, like me, were posing as patients. They felt safe because, on the block, selections were made only during the daytime hours, and at that time the functionaries were not among the sick.

Up to this point, there were five women working in the infirmary: two clerks, one nurse, one doctor, and one cleaning lady. I was designated as a third clerk. The important thing was that I should be someplace. Soon after I got there I met the girls I would be working with. Both of them were Slovak Jews. They were very religious and constantly had prayer books in their hands. Rachel, the older one, was the director of the Jewish Orthodox Slovak organization. Here in the camp she was able to create a strong group whose members carried out all of the religious commandments. The second clerk, Ada, was very young, and she obeyed her elder's orders scrupulously.

As soon as I got to know them, their fanaticism irritated me. Despite the reality that surrounded them, they continued to believe in the glory of the Chosen People. Here in Auschwitz, in the face of the unavenged murder of the whole Jewish people, in the light of the bestiality toward the elderly, women, and children, they continued to believe in God's special affection for the Jews. It was difficult for me to understand how they could maintain this belief in the face of the facts. Nevertheless, believe they did and remained faithful to their God.

The cleaning chores were handled by a Slovak girl named Magda. When I met her in February 1944, she was eighteen years old, but she had been in Auschwitz since 1941. She had the face of a madonna, with beautiful light hair and turquoise eyes. The camp degraded most women, but somehow it ennobled her. She was wonderful—very brave and also a happy girl. Later she became my camp daughter. Together we lived through many good and bad moments in Auschwitz, and for a short time in Ravensbrück.

The reception of the sick lasted until lunch time. After lunch Magda started working. She started by washing the tiles. Actually, this was a job that everybody participated in. While doing this, we joked around, sang, told stories in Czech, Slovak, and Polish— languages that all of us understood. At first I did not participate in the jokes and singing. I had not yet adjusted to the terror in the camp. The suffering and dying of those others whom I ran into at every step still did not just roll off my back. I had not yet cast off the thin skin of the *zugang*. This came later. Unless you sloughed off that skin you could not survive in Auschwitz.

We ate our lunch in a small room in the infirmary. The room was furnished with triple-decker beds, a few chairs, and a closet. Across from the door hung a mirror. For the first time since coming to Auschwitz, I had an opportunity to look at myself. I looked terrible. I did not resemble myself. I was sure that there was somebody else standing behind me and that the mirror was reflecting her face.

In the evening I went to the hospital ward where my sick card was located. I had to sleep there. It was after supper, and the block was very quiet, which bothered me. On both sides of the room there were triple-decker beds, and on every bed there were two sick women. My bed was at the end of the block. It was also a triple-decker. Two decks were taken by *nachtwache*. I took the third. Not far from my bed was a big stove that extended for the whole block. Two young Jewish girls from Poland had kindled a fire in the oven that first night and were cooking dinner in a pot. Through the whole block you could smell the aroma of potato soup and fried onions. They did not pay much attention to the sick. They opened the oven door and lazily warmed themselves.

Suddenly, with fright, I saw a few huge rats coming close to the stove. They had yellow fur and long tails. I let out a terrible shriek. The rats were unimpressed. They behaved like domestic cats. "You'll get used to it," said one of the girls. That night I dreamed that yellow rats were chewing on my throat.

WHAT KIND OF A PERSON WAS ORLI REICHERT?

Before I met Orli I had heard many different stories about her. Among the members of the anti-Fascist organization there was a wide range of opinion about this young, beautiful German who had been in prisons and concentration camps since 1933. As soon as Hitler came to power she was thrown into prison. At the time she was eighteen years old. She was sentenced to five years in prison for having been involved in some sort of manifesto. When the time came for her release in 1938, the Gestapo gave her a choice: either she could expose all the anti-Fascists with whom she had been in contact or she would spend the rest of her life in a concentration camp. Having refused to cooperate with the Gestapo, she was transported to various camps in Germany; following the occupation of Poland she was sent to Auschwitz. She was the most senior person in this death camp. She served as *lagerälteste* of the area. You could say, in plain language, that she held the lives of many women prisoners in her hands.

At the time I was in the camp I was fascinated by Orli's individualism. I must admit that even today I often think about her. She was a true German and yet a Communist at the same time. To what extent the camp demoralized her I cannot say. It seemed to me at the time that the Gestapo deliberately gave her power to undermine her ideals. They set her against the Communists of other nations who were struggling to survive in the Hell of Auschwitz.

I cannot judge Orli. I will not even try. I really do not understand her. I always saw her in a variety of situations, and in each situation she was a different person. On one occasion she would be defiant to the authorities; on another she would be cruel to the prisoners. At one moment she was filled with compassion for human suffering; at another, without blinking an eye, she made sure that not even one of the victims sentenced to the gas chamber would escape. On some days she was comradely with anyone who was fighting for freedom, no matter what the person's nationality. Yet there were times when she would isolate herself from the rest of us because she was German and it was her duty to support the German cause. For better or for worse Germany was her country.

I would like to describe her behavior toward various prisoners and, in doing so, arrive at some kind of judgment of her.

isten," Masha said to me, "I will tell you how Orli saved my life. In the summer of 1943 an epidemic of spotted typhus raged through the camp. There were days when three hundred sick people would report to the area with that dreadful disease. Piles of corpses littered the space in front of every hospital block. At first the Germans did not pay much attention to the epidemic. Apparently they thought that the disease would ravage only the prisoners. But the lice were so impudent that they took to biting the SS men. More and more SS men started coming down with typhus. At that point the camp administrators decided to take measures to stem the epidemic. In Auschwitz that did not mean treating the disease but rather burning the lice along with the people. Whole blocks of sick people went to the gas, and the nurses went with them.

"At that time I came down with typhus. Throughout the course of the sickness I continued to work. I walked around with a temperature of over 40 degrees, only half conscious. Eventually, the Germans found me out and put me on the typhus block. Since the whole block was made up of functionaries, people started deluding themselves that the Germans intended to spare this block. The first few days on the block I was unconscious and did not know what was going on around me. When I returned to consciousness a few days later I was informed that the whole block had been designated for the gas. At that time there were about three hundred sick people on the block. They were all young girls and were already convalescing. Some were actually completely healthy and were slated to leave the hospital the next day. But before anybody could leave, the block was sealed, and the only exit was through the chimneys of the crematorium.

"For three days we waited to be taken to the gas. I was so weak that I didn't care. The other girls, who had returned to health, were going absolutely crazy. They were all looking for some corner in which they could hide, although they knew very well that no such corner existed. They did not want to die. One afternoon they came to take some of the girls to the gas. The cars were parked in front of the block. The SS man stood on the stove and read out the numbers and the last names. The women had to get undressed right there on the block. Then the naked women were packed into the car. Some girls screamed, some ran away, some hid under the mattress. An SS man even shot one of them.

"Since my hearing had been impaired by my sickness, I listened very carefully to make sure I would hear my number. My life was so unpleasant to me I didn't even care about the gas. All I wanted to do was to avoid a beating. But I did not hear my number called. After everybody had left I was there alone. 'What is your number?' an SS man demanded. I showed him my hand. I didn't have the strength to speak. Bubi looked at it because the SS man was afraid to come close. 'You can stay here for the time being,' he said. 'Later, you will be transferred to the second block.' Then he went away. I was left alone on a big dead block. I was shivering so violently that I almost fell out of bed.

"In the evening Orli came, accompanied by some nurses. Later on the girls told me that Orli had demanded of Mengele—you know that renegade doctor—that he cross my number off the death list. She threatened to go to the gas with the Jews if he did not do what she asked. Mengele had a weakness for Orli. Moreover, she was a German and the director of the area. After some extended bargaining he finally crossed my number off the list. That's how Orli saved my life. If not for Orli, I would no longer be in this world."

A PLATE OF SOUP

Sonia came from the Ural Mountains. She had been in Auschwitz since 1943. She had come here straight from the front, one of a group of eleven nurses and one doctor—a surgeon known in Auschwitz as Dr. Lubow. They all managed to get to the area, but I do not really know how they all did it. The Russians were different from other prisoners. They were all broad, well built, and strong. Sonia was a very pretty girl, with a happy, smiling face. She was very kind. In fact, she was so good that she was somewhat helpless. It was dangerous to be too good in Auschwitz. As they say, in Auschwitz the pigs liked to feast on good people.

Sonia was a nurse on one of the blocks in the area. Orli knew her and respected her. I never heard Sonia criticize anybody and that includes Orli. But then again, Sonia really could not conceive the full range of Orli's behavior.

"When I first came to the area," Sonia told me, "I didn't expect to last for a week. At every step I encountered such horrible suffering that I couldn't bear it. I was used to helping people who were suffering. But what could I do here? It was hard for me to get oriented. From the moment I arrived on the area I admired Orli. In that sea of suffering she moved with confidence and self-assurance. She was able to decide who could be helped and who was to be sacrificed. Since you can't help everybody, you've got to know who can benefit from being helped and, of those who can benefit, who is most in need. Orli always knew." Sonia paused for a moment, as though looking for words that would express what she was feeling just then.

I remember thinking, during that interlude in Sonia's narrative, that in Auschwitz there was nothing more important than trying to help your fellow sufferers and yet, at the same time, how immoral it was to decide whose suffering should be alleviated and whose should continue unabated. Who had given us the right to condemn or to save another? In Auschwitz there was no fairness in the merciless struggle for survival. Those with scruples died isolated and abandoned. That was the new order of the concentration camp.

"Every day at noon we went to the kitchen," Sonia resumed her narrative. "As you know, the kitchen is far from the area, and the cans are heavy. When the Polish or French girls went to the kitchen, four girls carried the can. Vera and I went by ourselves, just the two of us. We still had our strength. You know how the prisoners mill around at lunchtime and what their faces look like." I certainly knew. Each would tie a string around the waist of her frock, and from the string there would always be a cup dangling. They were like famished dogs on the scent of a tasty morsel. They were like predators, crouched and ready to spring on their prey.

"Those prisoners milling around," continued Sonia, "were our plague. When they saw us carrying the cans, they would pounce from behind, open the cover, and before we could utter a word their cups would be in the soup. When we yelled they would run away, but in no time a new bunch would try the same trick all over again. By the time we got to the area the can was already half empty. I tried appealing to their consciences. 'How can you take food from the mouths of the sick? Did it ever occur to you that tomorrow we may be carrying soup for you?' Yelling and pleading did not help. They were hungry. That was their only argument. But when we brought a can half filled with soup, instead of one that was brimful, the result was that the sick, helpless women had to go hungry.

"Once Orli came with us to fetch the soup. 'I'll show you how to handle a matter like this in Auschwitz,' she said. She was known in the camp, and I was sure that the women would not dare to reach for the soup while she was around. Hunger was too strong a stimulus to be resisted. As usual, the hungry women were waiting for us. When the first two reached for the soup, Orli jumped out and pummeled them. You know how the functionaries distribute red cheeks and black eyes. After that, nobody bothered us, and we used to arrive on the hospital block with full cans of soup. I wouldn't condemn Orli just for that beating. It was what she told us after we had finally put the cans down on the block that bothers me. 'That's how you have to talk to people,' she told us, 'no other way. These people deserve no better.' At that time I thought to myself: 'Poor Orli. You really believe that in dealing with human beings a beating is the best argument.'"

ERIKA'S RED TRIANGLE

rika Schneider was a German. On the sleeve of her uniform she wore a four-digit number, which showed that she belonged to the earliest group of prisoners to arrive in Auschwitz, and above the number was a red triangle, which showed that she was a political prisoner. Erika was a dyed-in-the-wool Communist. She had been in prisons and camps ever since Hitler took power. When I met her in 1944 she was about forty years old. She was possessed of a young, sweet face set off by short, gray hair.

Erika did not like Orli. She criticized her attitude and her behavior, as well as her peculiar brand of communism. She reproached her weakness and denounced her for submitting to the SS men and for adopting their immoral attitude toward other human beings. Erika was a dogmatist not only in her appraisal of facts but, what was worse, in her appraisal of people. She overlooked the fact that Orli started her Golgotha as an eighteen-year-old girl. Orli had told us as much herself. She had gotten involved in the leftist movement, not for reasons of her own, but because her father and brother were members of the German Communist party. When Erika was arrested she was thirty years old, an agent of the Communist movement and a comrade of Mr. Thelman.

Erika was not a camp functionary, even though as a German she could have had a much easier life than the rest of us. "For that very reason," she used to say, "just because I am a German I want to share the fate of the pariahs of the camp." I must admit that Erika interested me. I was fascinated by that uncompromising communism and fanaticism, which sparkled with such a beautiful glow in this merciless world of Auschwitz. Once, as we were sitting in the darkness in the infirmary, we started to discuss Orli.

"Listen," Erika said to me. "I will tell you about one incident which will illustrate to you why I dislike Orli. A year ago there was a terrible selection in the area, which involved all of the hospital blocks. There was a prisoner on one of the blocks who was one of my dear friends. She was a Jewish girl from Germany. The girl, who was just recovering from pneumonia, was very weak. Her number had been written down by Mengele. I was distraught. In this one instance I decided to take advantage of my position as a German and to ask Mengele for a favor. You can imagine how much such behavior cost me.

"Mengele spoke to me politely. He told me to show up tomorrow, when they would be taking the people to the gas. I would be able to take care of the matter myself and would simply escort my friend away from the condemned group. I was very excited, and to tell the truth I suspected that Mengele was up to some kind of a diabolical trick. I never would have imagined that I would have come even this close to the bloody crime. But I had to go. It was a matter of a human life.

"Though it was July, it was a cool evening. Freight cars entered the area. They stopped in front of the blocks. Mengele stood to the side, and a slight distance from him stood Orli. As the SS men read the numbers, the women entered the cars, silent as shadows. Think! Orli was an accomplice to this heinous deed. Some young, skinny, tall girl tried to slip aside, and who do you think herded her to the car? Orli. I could hardly restrain myself from yelling out and spitting in her face.

"I stood as if mesmerized, unable to move from the spot. When Mengele saw me, he approached and said: 'Stand here, next to the car. When your friend comes out, point her out to me.' Apparently he was eager for me to see everything, especially the passivity of the people in the face of death. Suddenly I saw the friend for whom I had undertaken this torture beyond endurance. I started in her direction. Mengele called her. When she came close to Mengele he told her to remove her shirt and stand off to the side. I stood beside her. When the car was completely full, at the very last instant before the doors closed, he pushed her into the car. The train left, with her in it. I was glued to the spot. Mengele approached me and said, 'Understand this! I did it for her. She was too weak to live here. Why should she suffer?' I was struck with horror at the sudden realization that Orli was present at every selection and every death transport.

"When I discussed the situation with my friends the next day they told me that several comrades had been saved yesterday, thanks to Orli's actions. How could she save some and push others into the car of death?"

here were no roll calls in our area, but morning and evening we could see the roll calls taking place on the other side of the hospital wire, and we were glad that we did not have to stand for hours in the cold and the rain. So we were very surprised when one day the *blokowa* told us that we were going to have a roll call and that all the functionaries, doctors, and nurses would have to gather in front of the infirmary.

In Auschwitz we were panicked by any change in the routine. We knew from experience that change brought nothing good, and we accepted innovation only with the greatest trepidation. A few hundred people, everybody who worked on both the Jewish and Aryan blocks, gathered in front of the infirmary. The *blokowe* and *sztubowe* on one side, the doctors and nurses on the other.

"Achtung," shouted one of the *blokowe*, whereupon we all straightened up and stood at attention, waiting for the SS men. Orli walked slowly past the first row. She was alone. This was my first opportunity to get a close look at her. She was slight but powerful. She was wearing pants and a light sports jacket. She had brown hair, cut short in a masculine style. She walked deliberately along the length of the line, with her head hung low. Later she situated herself in front of the group and pulled a card out of her pocket.

"There won't be roll calls in this area. Don't be frightened. Today I gathered you all together because I want to read to you a complaint that the functionaries in the area wrote about me. The complaint is addressed to Dr. Mengele. This is it: 'Orli, our camp elder, surrounds herself with Communists and Jews. She gives all the jobs in the area to Communists. We do not want this situation to continue, and, therefore, we do not want Orli.' Are you curious as to what Mengele did with that letter? As you can see, he handed it over to me, and he asked me what the whole thing is all about. I told him that I am a Communist and that it is difficult for me to be friendly with whores. He told me to tear up the complaint, but I wanted to read it to you first. Now, I am going to tear it up. You are dismissed. But I would like to ask those who wrote the complaint, 'Aren't you ashamed to write such things to Mengele? I, a German, was ashamed for you today.'"

We left in silence and returned to our blocks. What kind of a person was Orli?

THE BLOCK OF DEATH

Rapportführer SS man Taube was famous in Auschwitz for his ability to kill a person in two motions. First he would hit the victim on the head to knock the person unconscious, and then he would put his foot on the person's throat strangling her to death. I remember being a witness to one of his executions on the *zugangen* block. One night Taube was in charge of the evening roll call, and that evening there was a number missing. The *sztubowe* were sent scurrying through the camp to look for the lost woman while I stood there trembling with fear to think what might happen to her when they found her. It turned out that she was in the camp latrine. She could not leave the place because she was suffering from dysentery. She was not yet aware of how important a cog she was in the camp mechanism, that they were not able to finish the roll call unless she was present. She had to be there, and the *sztubowe* had to drag her to appear before the *rapportführer*. It did not matter whether she were dead or alive. When the *sztubowa* hauled her to the roll call area she was half dead with fright. Taube approached her slowly and then snuffed out her life with his usual technique. It took no more than five seconds for Taube to perform the execution. After the execution we were permitted to return to our blocks. All numbers were accounted for, and the roll call was finished.

No one would tell me, and I asked often, why Taube, during the roll call of the first transport of Jews from Slovakia in 1941, should have noticed Cyla and appointed her to be *blokowa* of Number 25, the death block. Rosina, a nurse, and Mancy, a doctor from Bratislawa, told me stories about Cyla.

"Taube must have seen something terrible in Cyla," I said, "something that made her stand out from the other prisoners."

"Nothing of the sort," the girls answered. "She was almost a child when she first came to the camp. She was barely fifteen years old; when she was on the transport with us she was still wearing a school apron. She was slim, not too tall, and she was pretty. She came from a well-to-do, middle-class Jewish family, religious and highly respected. She had no brothers or sisters. Up to the moment that Taube told her to step out of the line and stand next to him, she was a normal girl, frightened as the rest of us by what was going on around her."

"Listen to how Taube made a criminal of her," Mancy started telling me. "He picked her out of the roll call, while she was dressed in rags, like the rest of the *zugangen.* Her head was shaved and she was wearing wooden shoes. That night she did not return to our block, so we were very worried about what might have happened to her. We did not know where they had taken her or what they were doing to her. Since we were all *zugangen*, it was impossible to find someone who could give us any information. Those first few months in the camp we had no contacts and no organization.

"For a few days Cyla was nowhere to be found. She was not on our block, and she was not with the *komando* working at the construction of the camp. We were sure that Cyla was no longer among the living. We could hardly imagine anything else. The first selection of the *zugangen* took place a few weeks after we arrived at Auschwitz. The murderous work in the swamps, the lack of wholesome drinking water, hunger, and disease knocked even the strongest prisoners off their feet. Young girls who had been the picture of health a few weeks earlier quickly became *mussulmen*, incapable of doing any work. The death camp was just being built at that time. The gas chambers, the crematoria, the *effektenkammer* were all being erected by the hands of the prisoners. Those who were not capable of hard work had to perish. At that time the selections took place at the roll call because the death machinery was not yet in working order. On that fall day of 1941, the day of the first selection, we stood at the roll call and waited for death.

" 'Achtung,' barked the *blokowa.* Taube walked into the roll call area, with Cyla following a short distance behind him. At first I did not recognize her. When finally I realized who she was I was so surprised that my eyes almost popped out. Could it really be Cyla? She looked so elegant and so scrubbed and she smelled so good. I looked her over, top to bottom. She wore rubbers on her feet, a beautiful rain coat, and a multi-colored silk scarf on her head. She avoided our gaze, looking straight in front of her. She walked behind the *rapportführer*, step for step. When he stopped she stood at his side. I was so fascinated at the sight of Cyla that I forgot about the selection. She stood to the side and waited patiently.

" 'Now you will stand in line and you will approach the *rapport-führer*,' shouted the *blokowa*. The line moved slowly, everybody trying to look her best. Every few minutes Taube picked somebody out of the line and stood her to the side. Then Cyla approached with a notebook in her hand and wrote down the number. The number of those standing off to the side began to swell. But all this time Cyla kept writing down the numbers, making sure that everybody remained in place. She did everything calmly and precisely. When the roll call ended, Cyla lined the women up in ranks of four and took the chosen ones to the new block. That was how the death block was created, and from that day Cyla was functioning as the *blokowa* there. Today she is eighteen years old and has the heart of a criminal capable of committing murder." That was the story Mancy told me.

Block 25 was located on field "A," not far from the block of the *zugangen*. From the outside it looked like any other camp block, except that it was always bolted, and people did not stroll around there. Those who chanced to be sent there left only in the *leichen-auto*, the car that transported the dead. Selections were a permanent feature of camp life. There were large selections, which encompassed the whole camp, and there were hospital selections, which Mengele arranged every few months. He always managed to arrange a selection when there was some Jewish holiday. When the holidays approached, we could expect a selection. Sometimes the selections reminded us that it was actually a Jewish holiday, which we would have forgotten otherwise. Mengele, that monster in the body of an Adonis, never forgot.

In addition to the large organized selections, a day did not go by that someone was not condemned to the gas. In our infirmary the SS doctors looked over the sick people who came to the area every day. It did not take long before we were able to tell which of the sick women would be sent to the gas. For example, Dr. Koenig did not like sick people with swollen feet. Mengele, on the other hand, did not like them with sores on their breasts. Since we knew in advance who would be looking over the women, we simply concealed those whom we knew would be vulnerable. Mengele gave us the most trouble. He was so handsome that he inspired trust. He would make himself comfortable in a chair and then become engrossed in conversation. The newly arrived women would forget where they were and start describing all their ailments.

One of them might tell him, "I have been suffering from a heart condition for a long time and I simply can't walk." Another might say, "The camp food doesn't agree with me, because I have liver problems."

These women did not realize that they were signing their own death warrants. Before the doctor's visit we would beg the women to say nothing and to pretend that they did not speak German, but rarely did anyone listen. Sometimes an SS man would write down the number of a prisoner to whom he had taken a dislike. There were times when for no reason at all, and contrary to the regular routine, several German doctors would descend on the block, look over the sick, and write down a few numbers for the gas.

All those whose numbers were listed went to the *blokowa*, whose duty it was to escort them to Block 25. Here Cyla received them, and from that moment forth they were nothing but meat for the oven. Strange as it may seem, the functionaries regarded those in Block 25 as dead already. I was once witness to this phenomenon. On one occasion, the clerk of one of the hospital blocks, a robust, healthy woman, took charge of the sick whose numbers had been written down during the selection. There were about thirty women in the group, all extremely emaciated. She gathered them together in the foyer, dressed only in their slips, then led them barefoot in the snow to the death block. She later explained this brutal procedure as follows: "I wanted to save myself some work. What is the point of taking them to Block 25 fully clothed, and then having to make an extra trip to the warehouse with their clothes. To them it doesn't matter anyway." I can still see the sad walk of those nearly naked women, holding each other up, leaving a trail of bloodstains in the snow. Beside them walked the red-cheeked clerk, dressed in a warm sweater, carrying in her hand the card containing the numbers of these corpses.

They stayed on the block until there were enough of them to fill the gas chamber so that the gassing could be carried out with maximum efficiency. Sometimes it took a few days, sometimes more. They waited for death. On Block 25, which it was forbidden to enter, Cyla had a little room. In the camp there were rumors circulated about the goings-on there. In her little apartment Cyla, it was rumored, received Taube, who was said to be her lover. Taube had issued orders that the sick on Block 25 were not to receive any food, thereby conserving the gas it would take to eradicate them. The result was that Cyla received a hefty portion of provisions because the sick were still on the camp register, and she would confiscate their rations for herself. Hot coffee was brought to the block in caldrons. Cyla would kick the caldron over, letting it spill into the drains, and then shout in several languages, "Drink water!" Her shouting could be heard all over field "A." Cyla exchanged margarine, bread, and salami for cigarettes. She would then exchange the cigarettes for luxuries that were brought into the camp by prisoners who worked outside the camp.

Cyla came to our infirmary very often. She was happy and very self-satisfied. She used to bring us chocolates, and once she even brought me a dress as a present. In spite of her cordiality I feared her greatly. To put it bluntly, she was a monster. I avoided getting into discussions with her. I remember that I once let my curiosity get the better of me, and I asked her the question that had been on my mind for a long time: "Tell me, Cyla, how can you act this way? Aren't you afraid that the people will never forgive you?"

We were alone in the infirmary, and no sooner had I popped the question than fear overwhelmed me. But she answered me calmly: "You probably know that I put my own mother in the car that took her to the gas. You should understand that there remains for me nothing so terrible that I could not do it. The world is a terrible place. This is how I take my revenge on it."

I did not see Cyla when the prisoners were evacuated from Auschwitz. I do not know what happened to her, but I am convinced that there can be no place for her among normal human beings.

isette had a strange face. It was as if it consisted of two elements that did not match. Her chin and jaw were sharp. You would think that they were those of a crude person, even an evil one. But her cheeks were round and flushed. She had an upturned nose, happy hazel eyes, and while I cannot remember the shape of her mouth, I do recall that there was always a cheerful smile on her lips. I must admit that her smile actually annoyed me. I met Lisette in Auschwitz in 1944, at the most dreadful period, when the sky over the camp was always red and the air reeked with the odor of burning flesh.

It was a macabre summer. There were times when I felt as though everything happening around me was unreal, that it must be the product of a sick imagination. Transports kept arriving day and night, and most of them went straight to the gas. Young, healthy women were instantly inscribed in the book of death. Completely naked, they were herded to an enclosure behind barbed wire. There they waited, under the July sun, without shade, without food, and without water.

The day was one marked by unusual bustle and activity. Trains arrived and departed. The Germans bellowed whenever someone tried to disrupt the established order, whenever someone failed to stand squarely in the line of death, whenever someone tried to hold on to a single valise that remained of all her possessions. All of the activity proceeded at a quickened tempo so that the people would not have a minute's respite during which they might stop to think and perhaps plan some opposition to their captors. "Schneller, schneller,"* the Germans barked, and the people running from the clubs and guns fell inevitably into the German whirlpool. At the very entrance to the bath house stood the camp doctor, the celebrated Mengele, beautiful, elegant, with a smile that inspired trust. With a careless motion of his hand he directed some to the right and some to the left. Women with children, old people, the

---

*"Faster, faster."

weak and the sick were on one side of the ramp. The young and healthy were on the other side. In front of Mengele everything was silent. There was no conversation. Everybody went in the direction casually indicated by the stick, not knowing that a verdict of life or death had just been pronounced on them. No one with a normal mind could comprehend this Hell.

Lisette went on walking through the camp with a cheerful smile on her lips, which drove me mad. We often discussed Lisette, especially with the girls from France, who knew her well. "How can she smile?" I asked. It gave me the creeps.

"I will tell you why she is smiling," Masha said to me. "She is just happy."

"What are you talking about? Happy?" I screamed, "Here in Auschwitz, happy? Is she blind and deaf to what is going on around her?"

"Don't interrupt me," said Masha. "If you let me talk I will explain everything. She is happy because her husband is not with her. When they arrested her he managed to run away, and now he is free. He is a wonderful young man. She loves him enormously. She also left her little daughter in freedom. Now she has only one thought in her head: how good it is that they are not in this Hell, that Mengele isn't telling them to go to one side or the other, that they are out of the reach of the Auschwitz murderers. When she thinks about that, a happy smile blooms on her lips."

I understood. From that time on, whenever I saw her smile, I winked, letting her know that I understood and that her smile did not bother me. Now I could share her happy secret.

I remember clearly that summer day in 1944 when Lisette stopped smiling. A transport of prisoners arrived from France, and among them was Lisette's husband. For a while the news that her husband was in Auschwitz was an unconfirmed rumor, and though Lisette did not believe it she tried to make certain one way or another.

She did not have to wait long. The prisoners who brought the laundry into the hospital brought a letter from him.

"I am with you," Karol wrote. "I would be happy, except for the *komando* I have been assigned to. Right from the transport I was assigned to the *komando* that works in the crematorium. I don't know what kind of work I will be doing, but I don't think I will be able to stand it here very long."

In the evening Lisette brought the letter to us so that we might read it. She was crazed with despair. Her beloved was in the lowest ring of Hell. The *komando* that worked in the crematorium lived only a few months. After a few months the Germans would liquidate the entire *komando* and choose a whole new set of people from the transports that were arriving in Auschwitz daily. They thought that in this way they would be able to bury the evidence of the atrocities they were committing here.

From this time on a letter from the crematorium would arrive every day, each time through a different channel.

"Dreadful," wrote Karol. "Today the men from the *komando* cooked soup for themselves in a pot which was supported by human bones. When I expressed my horror to them, they merely laughed."

"Dear Lisette," he wrote the next day. "Imagine, with the gold stolen from the people that have gone to the gas, the members of the *komando* buy liquor, sausage, and the best meats. Between the gassings they have drinking parties. I want to vomit when I see such things. They only laugh at me and say that a living corpse is not supposed to have scruples. I won't be able to hold out. I just can't cope with the situation. What shall I do?"

We read those terrible letters and tried not to look at Lisette, who grasped our hands and kept repeating, "Advise me, girls. Something must be done. I can't refuse his request for help. What is he supposed to do? How should he conduct himself those few months that he has to live?"

Later a letter came from him informing us that he had made his own decision. He had decided to commit suicide. "Forgive me, Lisette. I can't do any differently. I can't look at the bodies disfigured by pain that we drag out of the gas chambers, or at the suffering women and small children. I want to die. I don't want to be a witness to the baseness of human beings, as, for example, a son pushing his father into the ovens. That is what happens in our *komando*."

Then the anti-Fascist organization in Auschwitz, of which Lisette was a member and to which she now turned for help, made a momentous decision: "Let Karol organize a group from among the *komando* and let them blow up the crematorium. The organization will help."

The last autumn of Hitler's reign was approaching. The blowing up of one of the four crematoria that smoked day and night could not take place without creating an echo. It would instill courage in the prisoners, and the noise of the explosion would inform the people outside the camp of our fight. That is what most of us thought. But how did Lisette feel? For her, and she knew it very well, the exploding crematorium would announce the death of her husband.

Lisette was very calm. You could see her face turn to stone. She did not discuss the subject with us. Once she showed me a letter from Karol to the directors in which he agreed to carry out the project. Among other things, he had written, "I am so happy. Now I know why I am alive." I remember that at this point I wanted to correct the letter. To my way of thinking it should have said, "Now I have something to live for." I remember that day vividly when the crematorium was blasted into rubble. It was fall already, but warm and sunny, not golden, because there were no leaves in the camp to be gilded by the autumn sun. The time for the evening roll call was approaching. Suddenly a tremendous roar rent the air. I knew what it meant. Immediately the Germans announced a *blocksperre*—no one could leave the blocks. We stood at the half open gate and listened. From a distance we heard the screaming of the Germans and we heard shooting. We thought we heard the sound of people running away. A little later we heard the singing of the "Internationale," loud and clear, and sung in a mixture of languages. The dying greeted the revolution and announced the end of fascism. It sounded like the slogan with which the gladiators traditionally greeted Caesar: "Caesari, morituri te salutant"—"Caesar, those about to die salute you." Then there was more shooting, more screams, and finally a resounding silence.

The evening roll call started. As usual, the *komandos* came through the gate, and as usual the camp orchestra was playing. All of the women kept their heads bowed so that the SS men would not be able to read the joy sparkling in their eyes. We were proud of those who had died as heroes. How different it was from the dying that we were witness to day after day.

It was dark when Masza rushed into the infirmary. "A doctor. Quick, a doctor! Lisette's cut her veins." We all ran. When we got there she was already bandaged. She was lying on the bunk, pale, with the old smile on her lips. "He is not here in this Hell. He left," she kept repeating over and over.

MARIE AND ODETTE

Odette was French. She was brought to Auschwitz in January 1944. At that time I was still on the block for newcomers. Odette was about fifteen years old, and her mother could not have been older than thirty. They resembled each other, and the mother was young enough so that they looked like sisters. They were both very pretty—slim, with brown eyes and prominent mouths. Since they spoke only French they did not understand the orders that the *sztubowa* barked at them, and as a consequence they absorbed many a beating. On several occasions I served as their interpreter; it was perhaps for that reason that they trusted me.

Marie—that was the mother's name—was a seamstress. Odette was still a student. They were Parisians. The husband had been shot very soon after the Germans entered Paris. I did not ask why they were arrested. They did not have to confide in me.

One evening, she said to me, "You probably think that they arrested Odette and me because of my activities. Would you believe that it was my little Odette who was fighting against the Germans? I don't know how they happened to get on her trail, but when they came to arrest her I let them take me. It didn't work. They just waited in the house for somebody else to show up. When Odette came they took her too. To this day they don't know who's who. That's how we escaped one severe beating. This way we share the beatings. Now we are in Auschwitz, which we won't be able to survive, because I have a weak heart and Odette is too brave."

Meanwhile, I envied them because they were together. When they cuddled up together, lying on the hard bed, they must have dreamt that they were together in their own home. They went through the selection. Later on, when I went to the hospital I failed to see them.

The spring of 1944 was cold and ugly. I remember how we yearned for warm weather. It was not absolutely vital to us, but we hoped for warm weather for the sake of the women who were coming to the infirmary with frost bite on their arms and legs.

Many of them had pneumonia but continued to work. They were afraid to go to the hospital ward because very often selections were carried out there.

I worked in the infirmary, but at night I slept on the hospital ward, where I was registered as a patient. Usually I came to the block late, after supper. The light was dim, the air full of groans and heavy with misery and suffering. That evening I returned earlier than usual; it was not even supper time yet. The *blokowa*, who treated me as an equal, met me at the entrance. She took my arm, and we returned to the block together. She was making her evening rounds. I stood at my bed.

Suddenly I heard terrible shouting coming from the *blokowa*. How they could scream! Shouting was the symbol of leadership in the camp, so they were always screaming at the top of their lungs. Later I heard the sound of a beating taking place, accompanied by a weak voice of protest. I approached the direction from which the sounds were coming. Odette was standing in front of the *blokowa*, red as a beet. Her mother lay on the bed next to her.

"Tell them that this is my mother," she cried out in anguish. "They don't want to believe me. This is my mother. My mother."

The new arrivals had been taken to field "B," and from there they had been taken to the *komando* that was working in the *unionfabrik*, a munitions factory. The work was very difficult; the mother fell ill.

"Her heart, her sick heart," sobbed Odette.

For a week the mother had been lying in the hospital, and she was getting weaker every day.

"What shall I do? How can she be saved?"

Odette grabbed my hands and looked into my eyes, waiting for me to give her an answer.

I could only help her by coming to visit them in the evening. They whispered endearing words to each other, because Odette could not bring her anything else. Mancy examined Marie thoroughly and confirmed that she would not be able to survive in Auschwitz. Every morning, when the *komando* was on its way to work, and was waiting as usual at the exit gate, Odette would storm into the area and go straight to the block where her mother was lying. She said, "Good morning," kissed her mother, hugged her, and was gone. She had to catch up with her *komando* at the gate.

I remember the exact night that Marie died. Odette came at her usual time, and it was just after she left that Marie started feeling bad, and in a few minutes she was no longer alive. In the morning the *sztubowa* walked around the block, dragging out the dead. Their shirts were taken off and their naked bodies were thrown in front of the block. Later, the *leichenkomando* would collect the dead from the side of the block and stack them in a big pile near the infirmary.

That day snow and rain were coming down, and Marie's corpse lay rotting in the mud in front of the block. Although her body had grown emaciated while she was alive, in death she appeared beautiful. I wanted to put the body someplace else before Odette came running in, as was her custom, to see her mother, but there was no other place. I could not return her to her bed because it was already occupied by another sick woman, and I could not put a corpse in bed with the other women. I tried to lay the corpse in the foyer, but the *blokowa* almost beat me for that. Once again Marie was lying in front of the block. I could not wait for Odette. I simply did not have the strength. I did not want to be there when she first caught sight of her dead mother, naked and covered with snow and mud.

I went to the infirmary. Maybe Odette would not come today, I thought, and by evening the mother would no longer be in front of the block. From a distance I kept an eye on the gate of the area. The gate creaked, and there was Odette running with all her might. She got to the block, and after a minute she ran out. Apparently they had told her about her mother's death. She stood in front of the block, and there saw her mother. She sank down onto the snow and let out a scream so penetrating that I can still hear it to this day. She sat there for a few minutes and then fell on her mother's corpse. Finally, she arose and ran to the *komando*. She had to be on time at the gate. Poor little Odette. She was now alone in this terrible world.

Odette did not come to the area any more. She lived on the

second field, and I did not know what was happening to her. If she was not in the area that must mean that she was healthy. She had probably found a good friend in the *komando* where she worked.

It was the end of October 1944. We were still inspired by the heroic *sonderkomando* who had blown up one of the crematoria. In the evening that was the only thing we talked about. We did not know whether all of them had died or whether some had managed to escape. Late into the long nights of that October we could hear the barking of dogs. Evidently the SS men were looking for somebody. Several days after the event we heard the terrible news. Four young girls from the *unionfabrik* had been arrested on the charge that they had delivered the explosives used to blow up the crematorium. Odette was one of those arrested.

They were confined in a bunker where they were being tortured. They did not betray anyone. We knew that they must die. But what kind of death would the Germans cook up for them?

On a dark and rainy day, after all the *komandos* had returned from work, the four girls were hung on the gate, next to the sign, "Arbeit macht frei."* Marie rightly foresaw the death of her daughter: "She is too brave to live in Auschwitz." Brave, but naïve.

*"Work makes you free."

ESTHER'S FIRST BORN

April 1944 was unusually sunny. In the air you could feel the warm breezes of spring. This year, in the neighborhood of the railroad tracks that led straight to the crematorium, the women were at work laying sidewalks and arranging bunches of flowers. The earth, which smelled of freedom, was freshly dug, and hope entered our hearts. Not far from the fence, new earth was piled up and topped with a floor. This was where the camp orchestra gave concerts and singers sang famous solos. Once a week, after lunch, those concerts took place in the area. Anyone who could drag his feet came. Benches were taken out of the barracks. The healthier people stood or sat on the ground. Those who were able to get to the concert listened, and their thoughts would escape far beyond the present stinking, sordid life.

The orchestra consisted of many instruments. The conductors were a Russian woman and a Hungarian woman. A beautiful Hungarian woman was the soloist. The members of the orchestra wore identical outfits, and the soloist even wore an evening gown. I can remember one of those red, low-cut dresses in which she did not hesitate to appear for the performance. The Russian girl was young—very poised and calm. As soon as she tapped with her baton, the Strauss waltzes started flowing immediately. Everything looked so innocent, but we who knew how much human misery, degradation, and suffering were being covered by this curtain of music, and how many shattered dreams were there, were startled by this seeming innocence. The second conductor was dark and fiery. She also played the violin, and as she played she turned one way and another, setting the rhythm of a czardas for the orchestra, which accompanied her as she played the longing notes of a gypsy melody.

Sometimes, near the barbed wire, a train would go by, carrying Jews from the west in Pullman cars. The people tried to get to the window to wave to us. They took in the ideal picture, which calmed them and allowed them to believe that they were really going to work and that there would even be time for play. I lowered my head, realizing that I was taking part in this deception that was helping the Germans to send millions of people, without difficulty, to a torturous death.

One warm April day Esther came to the infirmary. She approached me and said very quietly, "I have a very important matter to discuss with you. Can we discuss it privately?"

I knew Esther from the Bialystok Ghetto. On 16 August 1943, the Bialystok Ghetto had been liquidated. For three months Esther, her husband, her mother, and a five-year-old niece who perished in Slonim,* hid with me in a bunker built in my apartment. At the time she was a young woman. I doubt that she was even twenty years old. She had a pretty face but it was not an interesting one. I remember that in the bunker we had a lot of trouble with her, because she had no talents and could not be counted on to help out. When the German gendarmes discovered our bunker they shot her husband on the spot. As soon as the three females arrived at Auschwitz, the Germans took away the little girl whom she had cared for affectionately, and a few months later her mother was taken at a selection. Esther was alone in Auschwitz.

She stood before me, now, peculiarly thick, red in the face and a little embarrassed. Maybe she was pregnant.

"As you can see for yourself," she blurted out, "I am going to give birth any day now. All this time I've been going to work, but now I want to stay in the hospital. I want to give birth to this baby. It's my first baby. It moves. It kicks me. It will probably be a son. My husband is not here anymore. That's his son. Please help me," she ended her pleading.

I turned to stone. Didn't she know what Mengele did to women who had babies in the camp? I looked into her happy eyes and at her enraptured features. For the first minute I really did not know what to tell her. Could I extinguish the happiness that emanated from her whole body? Or maybe I should just say nothing. Maybe I

*A small city in eastern Poland with a substantial but fluctuating Jewish population before World War II. Ruled by Poland between World War I and World War II, it was captured by the Germans on 17 July 1941.

should let her live through her great love for her first baby and let the worst come later.

Orli had told me once how Mengele explained to her why he killed Jewish women together with their children. "When a Jewish child is born, or when a woman comes to the camp with a child already," he had explained, "I don't know what to do with the child. I can't set the child free because there are no longer any Jews who live in freedom. I can't let the child stay in the camp because there are no facilities in the camp that would enable the child to develop normally. It would not be humanitarian to send a child to the ovens without permitting the mother to be there to witness the child's death. That is why I send the mother and the child to the gas ovens together."

Imagine that cynical criminal justifying his hideous crimes in the name of humanitarianism, making a mockery of the tenderest of all feelings, a mother's love for her children.

I had seen the conditions under which Jewish women gave birth in the camp. A doctor from the infirmary took me to one of the births. "Come with me," she said. "Join me in witnessing the crimes of Auschwitz and the depths of human suffering."

On our way to the block in field "B" Mancy told me that the women who were due to deliver were not taken to the infirmary. The delivery took place in the block where the woman lived. "You see," she said, "the birth has to take place in secrecy. Nobody is supposed to know about it. In the hospital block it is impossible to conceal the birth of a child from the Germans. Our procedure now is to kill the baby after birth in such a way that the mother doesn't know about it."

"What? You kill it?" I stopped in the middle of the path.

"It's very simple," Mancy continued. "We give the baby an injection. After that, the baby dies. The mother is told that the baby was born dead. After dark, the baby is thrown on a pile of corpses, and in that manner we save the mother. I want so much for the babies to be born dead, but out of spite they are born healthy. I simply don't know why the children are healthy. The pregnant women do heavy work till the last day; there is no food; and in spite of it all, the children are healthy. My worry now is that I don't have any injections left."

It was already dark when we arrived at the block. The women took us to the woman in labor. Mancy told her to lie on the ground under the board bed. She herself hid there too. "Remember," she said to her quietly, "you are forbidden to utter a sound. Everything has to take place in complete silence. Nobody should know that you are giving birth." She told me to bring her a bucket of cold water. She put it next to her.

"Sit next to me. You will be my helper," she said to me.

Two women stood near the bed. One of them was guarding the entrance to the block.

The birth started. The woman bit her lips in pain until she drew blood. But she did not utter even one sound. She held my hands so tightly that afterwards I had black and blue marks. Finally, the baby was born. Mancy put her hand over his mouth so he would not cry, and then she put his head in the bucket of cold water. She was drowning him like a blind kitten. I felt faint. I had to get out from under the bed.

"The baby was born dead," Mancy said. Later, she wrapped the dead baby in an old shirt, and the woman who was guarding the entrance took the baby and left to put it on a pile of corpses. The mother was saved.

Right then Esther, who knew nothing, was standing in front of me, wanting to go to the hospital to give birth to a baby like thousands of other women in the world. She was listening to the movements of her baby and was happy. She did not know that if a German doctor found out she would die with her baby. I decided to tell her everything.

"You see, Esther," I started, "you can't give birth to a living baby. It must die before anybody finds out about it. Otherwise, you will die with it."

"What? A dead baby? I want to have a live baby. I am sure that when Mengele sees it he will let me raise it in the camp. It is going to be a beauty because my husband was very handsome. You knew him. I want to have it in the infirmary."

Mancy and Marusia talked to her, but without success. The

same day she went to the infirmary, and that night she gave birth to a beautiful baby boy.

She lay there in bed with the baby, very happy. The attendants tried to convince her not to feed the baby so that it would die of hunger. Esther would not hear of it. She gave the baby her breast and talked with wonder about how beautifully it suckled. The supervisor of the infirmary had a duty to report all births, but somehow she delayed. She had pity on Esther.

On the third day of Esther's stay in the hospital block, the first day of the Passover holiday, a big selection took place. I was on the block when Mengele and an SS man came in. They both stood on the stove. The gate was bolted, and every sick woman was paraded naked in front of them. In his tightly closed fist Mengele held a pencil whose point stuck out a little way from his palm. The SS man read, and at the same time, wrote down the numbers, while Mengele pushed the pencil into his fist with a slow movement of his thumb. This meant death. The red-headed SS man put down a cross next to the designated number. Finally, Esther's turn came. She went naked, and in her arms she held the baby. She held it up high as though she wanted to show them what a beautiful and healthy son she had. Mengele slowly pushed the pencil into his clenched fist.

OLD WORDS—NEW MEANINGS

or some people, Auschwitz was an ordinary term, but now the word had taken on a completely new set of meanings. An unusually interesting psychological study might result if someone could demonstrate the way in which meanings passed beyond the accepted boundaries of conventional significance. Why a psychological study? Because the new set of meanings provided the best evidence of the devastation that Auschwitz created in the psyche of every human being. No one was able to resist totally the criminal, amoral logic of everyday life in the concentration camp. To some extent all of us were drawn into a bizarre transformation of reality. We knew what those innocent words meant, such words as "gas," "selection," but we uttered them, nevertheless, as though there was nothing hidden behind them.

Take the word "organize." Usually it is associated with such positive values as political, social, and cultural order and well-being. When we say of someone that he is a good organizer we usually mean that he is a constructive leader who brings sanity and tranquility to the whole community. In Auschwitz, however, "to organize" meant to improve your own situation, very often at someone else's expense by taking advantage of that person's ignorance or inexperience. "To organize" meant to procure for yourself, by any means, better clothing, lodging, or food. The person who knew how "to organize" slept under a silk comforter, wore silk underwear, and had not only enough bread and soup but even meat. How did she do it? I thought about it after I saw how she had prospered. When I first met her she was in tattered rags. Now she wore warm boots and an elegant sweater. She had a full belly and a smile on her face. When I asked the other prisoners about her I kept getting the same answer: "Apparently she knows how to organize." I managed to observe the workings of this kind of "organizing" in the young lady from Cracow named Fela.

In January 1944 we were both inmates in the new arrivals block. Eighteen years old at the time, she had been sent to Auschwitz when she was caught smuggling food into the ghetto for her family. She was a tall, slim girl with very light blond hair. She was not a beauty, but she had a quality that was impossible to describe. Something forced you to look at her. She was alone, without family or friends, but in spite of that, she did not give the impression of being helpless. She looked around attentively as though looking for some way to put her past experience to use. She did not cry, and she was not dismayed by the things that were taking place around her. She analyzed the situation carefully as if she were calculating how to establish herself most comfortably. An aura of self-assurance radiated from her whole being. This self-assurance allowed her to move freely without cramping her style in any way.

Fela did not talk to anyone. She was always alone. That girl interested me very much. I tried to get closer to her but she would not even stop for me. It was only after one of the selections, when she saw that I had protectors, that she reconsidered, deciding, apparently, that my acquaintance could be useful. One evening she came to talk to me.

"Taking everything into account," she said, "is it really that bad for everybody in Auschwitz? *Blokowe*, wardens, and many other people who are hangers-on are living very well. They will certainly live through Auschwitz. I am trying to figure out how to get myself into that group. I have to think of something to avoid being a victim who is always hungry and who is always being beaten by everybody. I have to find a way out, and I'm sure I will."

The girl amazed me. She spoke about the weak, persecuted, and hungry women with such contempt. Such a lack of all scruples in a girl barely eighteen years old was something unusual.

"I have to organize something. I have to see to it," she ended.

That was the first time I heard the term "to organize" in the new Auschwitz sense. After that talk I did not see Fela for a long time. We had been working in different areas, but one evening we met by chance. I had almost forgotten about her when I met her that evening on the hospital block. She was carrying a sack full of bread. Our chance encounter took her aback a little, but only for one short moment.

"What are you doing here," I yelled angrily. "Is this what your 'organizing' looks like? Is it part of your 'organizing' to steal bread from the sick? Get out of here quickly, before I call the head of the block!"

But Fela did not run away. She stood there, waiting for my anger to disappear.

"Now I will tell you where I got the bread," she said after a minute. "It is a long and not so simple story. 'You steal the bread,' you said. I didn't steal it, I earned it."

There was a pause, but I did not question her. I waited for further explanation.

"There was a woman from my *komando* lying on this block. One evening I came to see her and brought her a cup of potato soup cooked with one measly potato. You should have seen how she ate it, and how the other women who were lying next to her begged me to cook some soup for them. The next day, after the evening assembly, I went to the back of the kitchen with my portion of bread, which I had not eaten. I was looking for the woman who was working at the potatoes, in the hope that she would trade some potatoes for my bread. I found the woman, who gave me seven potatoes and a small onion for one portion of bread. I went into the block, and in a big tin can that I had brought with me from work, I cooked a potato soup with the seven potatoes. I fried the onion in my portion of margarine and put it into the soup. The soup smelled good. It was hot and fresh. I went to the hospital and sold the soup to the sick. I got a portion of bread for a cup of soup. They couldn't eat that dry bread, and the rats wound up taking it right from under their pillows. That very first evening I took in five portions of bread. You yourself must admit that I didn't steal the bread but earned it. The next time I earned four portions, and today I got fourteen portions of bread for the soup."

I stood there facing her, not knowing what to say to her or how to act toward her. It was certainly an ugly way of "earning" bread, taking it from unfortunate, very sick women, tearing the very last bite out of their mouths. But that is what they wanted. They preferred this cup of watery soup smelling of home to the portion of stale bread. To throw Fela out of the hospital would be to deprive the women of the soup for which they had been waiting all day. Nobody else would "organize" the soup.

"Ask the sick," she said, as though reading my mind. "Ask them whether they want the soup or not. See what they say."

I already knew for certain that I was not going to tell the head of the block and that Fela would continue to sell her soup to the sick.

"What are you doing with the bread?" I looked at the sack full of bread. "Don't tell me that you're going to eat fourteen portions of bread all by yourself."

"I don't eat it all. I exchange some of it for cigarettes. There is somebody I meet at work who gives me cigarettes for bread. You know, for cigarettes you can buy anything in the camp: clothes, good food, even good work. I have to give some cigarettes to the *blokowa* and, what is more important, some to the *sztubowe* so they won't interfere. But there are still enough left for me. I can get good food and good clothes. I can even bring something for you. I am collecting cigarettes now because I want to get good work. I have something particular in mind."

Fela left. That night I pondered our encounter and the moral problems that Fela had set before me. How could I evaluate her behavior? In Auschwitz she would have earned an A+. But what grade would Fela have earned if her behavior were viewed within a larger perspective?

A few weeks went by. It was lunch time when, from the main road, there came the sound of a German song pounded out to the rhythm of bootsteps. I went out in front of the infirmary. It was the marching of the *komando* who worked in the *effektenkammer*, commonly known as *kanada*. In *kanada* things brought to Auschwitz by Jews from all over Europe were sorted out. All of them thought that they were going to work, that they would work and live. People took all of their best things with them. The Germans allowed them to take only one valise and one knapsack. People packed gold and jewelry, furs and their best clothes. Now, the girls from the *effektenkammer* worked at unpacking the valises, sorting and shipping the goods to Germany. Only the young and pretty girls were chosen for this *komando*. They wore red kerchiefs on their heads and belts that were made especially to each girl's measurements. They had it good. A fortune passed through their hands. No wonder they lived in comfort.

They paraded to lunch in fours to the accompaniment of a marching song. I looked at them from afar and thought that, if I were to see their picture in a newspaper, I would have had a hard time believing that they were prisoners in the death camp of Auschwitz. Those singing prisoners were part of the system of the death factory. Suddenly, one of the marching girls caught my eye. It was Fela. She noticed me from afar. She tore the red kerchief from her head and waved happily to me. This was the good work she was dreaming about when she had collected the bread for the cups of hot soup that reminded the dying women of the taste of home. With that bread, which she had then exchanged for cigarettes, Fela got the job in *kanada*. Now she no longer carried soup to the hospital block. She was too busy with other higher-paying transactions.

A few more weeks went by. One evening Fela came to the infirmary. She walked in very quietly, without her usual self-assurance. Was it possible that she was not working in *kanada*? She had brought me a present, a beautiful nightgown. I knew that she wanted to tell me something, but she did not know where to start. We were quiet for a long time.

"Don't you work in *kanada* anymore?" I threw the first line from the shore.

She was still working there, but terrible things were happening. Even for her they were terrible.

"Imagine. I unpack a valise, and I find a dead girl in it. She must have been about two years old when she died. I was terribly disturbed. The girls told me that they often find dead children in the valises. The mothers hid the children in the hope that once they got them into the camp they and the children would remain together. Later, the valises were taken from them and brought to us, but by that time the children were no longer alive. I can't forget about it. I can't help thinking that all those beautiful clothes belonged to people who are no longer living. The girls say that this feeling will pass, that I will get used to things and forget about it. I don't know whether I'll be able to stand it there. It's worse than the business with the soup," she said at the end.

A few weeks went by again. Fall had arrived. A cold rain was falling outside. The mud was so thick and clinging that it was difficult to walk between the blocks. That evening, in addition to the regular staff, we had a visitor, Kwieta, a good friend of Marusia's, who worked in the *leichenkomando*. She was waiting for the car that was to pick up the dead bodies that were heaped in a huge pile. Suddenly we heard the roar of the car, and Kwieta jumped up from her seat in order to get to the pile of corpses. The entire *komando* was supposed to help load the car. Kwieta did not have a chance to leave the infirmary. The door opened with a crash, and in staggered a peculiar figure covered with soot and wrapped in a blanket. Behind her appeared an SS man. "The driver of the dead," Kwieta whispered.

"Do something with her," he said. "She will tell you everything."

He came in. The peculiar figure tumbled to the floor. It was Fela. Except for the blanket she had nothing on. She was naked and covered with ashes. Mancy and Marusia revived her. Later, we washed her up, dressed her, and fed her. Then Fela started her unusual story.

"Two weeks ago I fell sick with pneumonia. I was in the hospital and was recovering. The day before I was supposed to go back to *kanada* to work, Mengele wrote down my number for the gas. I found myself on the death ward. Yesterday the car came to take us to the crematorium. I didn't want to die. I was looking for a way out. All of a sudden, I saw something like a chimney jutting out of one side of the car, and I got into it. 'Maybe they won't see me,' I thought. Later, I figured out that the car ran not only on gasoline but also on wood.

"The car went to the crematorium. The women were chased into the gas chambers. I remained in the chimney unnoticed. The empty car returned to the garage. I was in the garage alone. Covered with soot and without any clothes, I got out of the car. That's how I spent the night. I didn't know what I would say when the SS man returned. In the morning he came and was terribly frightened when he saw me. He probably believed in devils and thought that I was a creature not of this earth. After I told him the whole story, he brought me a blanket and food and told me to sit there till evening, when he would be going for the dead. Then he would take me back to the women's camp."

The next day we did not report the death of a woman who had died that day, and Fela took her place on the register of the area.

She left Auschwitz with the next transport. I do not know whether she "organized" further. I never saw her again.

CHILDREN

he summer of 1944 was the worst of times. The death factory in Auschwitz was working at a frantic pace. Day and night trainloads of people were unloaded on the ramps. Most of them went directly to the gas chambers.

The infirmary was located near the ramp, and though we were not allowed to leave the block, we managed, through the crack of the open gate, to see what was going on. On one occasion a freight train with a long line of locked cars arrived at the ramp. The SS men and the prisoners who made up the *sonderkomando* were already waiting at the track. The train stopped and the doors opened with a loud roar. A horde of weary, exhausted souls carrying valises, rucksacks, and an assortment of packages spilled out onto the tracks. Now the *sonderkomando* sprang into action. They threw themselves on the valises, rucksacks, and packages, tearing them out of the tightly clenched fists of the new arrivals and tossing them to the side. Some people tried to protect their possessions. They explained to the SS men that the things in the valises were necessities. How would they be able to live without them? One SS man listened to their protestations, standing there with his legs spread wide. Then he uttered a shout and cracked his whip, thus reminding the new arrivals of their situation. Their complexions turned gray. They hunched their shoulders and obediently took their places in the death line.

Women and children also got off the train. Often the little girls would be holding dolls in their arms, while the little boys in short pants were jumping and running after a ball. The children did not seem to be as tired as the adults. They looked around curiously, satisfied at finally having left the dark wagons. The mothers and children were put in one line that passed slowly in review before the searching eyes of Mengele.

When I looked at those women and children brought here from such great distances for this torturous death, I always reminded myself of a colony in the Kingdom in *Pustyni i Puszczy* (*The Desert and the Wilderness*) by Henryk Sienkiewicz. When two war-

ring African tribes were engaged in a life and death struggle, the
women and children were placed in a sheltered colony where
they were completely safe and none of the combatants was permitted to enter. The women and children of both tribes were beyond the hate of the opposing tribes. Here in Auschwitz the German thugs murdered women and children first. The imagination
can conceive no penance that would atone for the bestial crimes
that the Fascists perpetrated on innocent individuals. What might
the Fascists answer if Humanity should ask: "Why did you throw
living Jewish children from Hungary into the flames? Why, on a
single October night, did you send all the gypsies to the ovens?
Why did you condemn the Polish children from Zamosc to freeze
to death?"

A LIVING TORCH

very day of that macabre last summer of Hitler's reign twenty thousand people were killed in Auschwitz. The crematoria were unable to burn all of the dead who were being gassed in Auschwitz. Large ravines were excavated next to the crematoria. The dead bodies were thrown into them, and then they were doused with benzine and set aflame. The flames leaped upwards, and the sky was turned red by the gigantic fire. At night the entire scene looked grotesque. We would go out to the front of the block and stare at the reddened sky. We were not so much mesmerized by the flames as by the sea of human blood. Burning human flesh gives off a sweet, choking odor that makes you feel faint. That summer we were saturated with that indescribable choking odor. All summer we groped our way around in the smoke that belched from the chimneys of the crematoria above and from the burning bodies in the ravines below. That July and August the weather was very hot and stuffy. It was a terrible summer. Looking back, now, it is difficult for me to say how we were able to live through those times, conscious of human life oozing out of existence everywhere. How is it that we did not all go crazy? How is it that we were able to vegetate, keeping our composure in this unbearable world? The time arrived when a scream tore itself involuntarily out of one's throat.

We were standing, as was our wont, in front of the block, watching the sky turn to a deeper red. All around us was quiet that night, because there was no transport. Apparently there was a large backlog of corpses that had to be burned before the new raw material essential to the functioning of the death factory could be brought in. Suddenly, the stillness was broken by the screaming of children, as if a single scream had been torn out of hundreds of mouths, a single scream of fear and unusual pain, a scream repeated a thousand times in the single word, "Mama," a scream that increased in intensity every second, enveloping the whole camp and every inmate.

Our lips parted without our being conscious of what we were

doing, and a scream of despair tore out of our throats, growing louder all the time. The *blokowa* and the *sztubowa* chased us into the block and threw blankets over us to smother our screams. They were afraid that our despair would communicate itself to the rest of the women, those who lay sick and dying in this oppressive hospital block.

Finally, our screaming stopped. On the block we could still hear the screams of the children who were being murdered, then only sighs, and at the end everything was enveloped in death and silence. The next day the men told us that the SS men loaded the children into wheelbarrows and dumped them into the fiery ravines. Living children burned like torches. What did these children do to suffer such a fate? Is there any punishment adequate to repay the criminals who perpetrated these crimes?

THE LITTLE GYPSY

The German doctors used to come about twelve o'clock. They would look over the sick who had checked into the hospital that morning, and then sign the so called *beff-karte*, which amounted to a permit to remain there for a day. Later, we were on our own. We cleaned and prepared dressings for the evening when the *komando* returned from work. At such times we felt a little less tense.

We were sitting in a little room in the infirmary when Marusia yelled, "Achtung!" We jumped up quickly and ran inside. We were standing at attention when Mengele walked in with a little gypsy boy who may have been about four years old. The little boy was a beauty. He was dressed in a gorgeous white uniform, consisting of long pants with an ironed-in crease, a jacket adorned with gold buttons, a man's shirt, and a tie. We stared, as if bewitched, at that beautiful child. It was clear that Mengele was pleased to see us thus enchanted. He placed a chair in the middle of the infirmary and sat down in it, keeping the little gypsy squeezed between his knees. The little boy understood German.

"Show them how you dance the *kozak*," he said. The little one danced the *kozak* while Mengele clapped his hands in rhythm. The little one kicked up his heels while maintaining a sitting position. He was astonishing. "Now sing a song." The little one sang a haunting gypsy melody.

We continued to stand at attention while the little one was showing off in front of Mengele. You could see that Mengele liked him. He hugged him and kissed him. "That was beautiful. Here is something for the performance," he said, taking a box of chocolates out of his pocket. They left. We looked at each other, not understanding why Mengele brought the boy to us. Why did he want to exhibit the child's talent to us?

"I am sure that Mengele will kill him soon," Marusia said.

We felt a cold chill.

The whole summer Mengele paraded around the camp with the little gypsy, who was always dressed in white. Even when the selections took place, the beautiful little boy dressed in white stood at his side. There was a family camp for gypsies in Auschwitz on field "C." There were twenty-five thousand gypsies in the camp. The children lived together with their families. It is hard for me to say why they opened the family camp in Auschwitz, why they permitted the gypsies to believe that they would be allowed to live through the war. In the fall of 1944, the end came for the gypsy camp. I don't remember the exact date, but the liquidation took place one October evening. In the morning all the young gypsy women were taken. As they were being herded to the transport the women cried bitterly. Evidently they understood that those who were staying in the camp were condemned to death. It was true. The same evening you could hear the murmur of the engines. They were all taken to the gas chambers. In that one night, twenty thousand gypsies were murdered.

It is peculiar. But throughout that whole slaughter we could think of only one. Was Mengele going to protect the beautiful boy from the gas? The next day he paraded through the camp without the little gypsy. The men told us that at the last minute Mengele had pushed him into the gas chamber with his own hands.

TAUT AS A STRING

Karola was a registered nurse. Before the war she had worked in a hospital in Krakow. If it is true that the practice of a profession influences a person's outward appearance as well as a person's psyche, then Karola was an excellent example of the rule. All you had to do was to take one look at her and you would instantly know what her profession was. The tranquil expression on her face, the calmness of her movements, her quick, light step, and the nobility of her figure all indicated that Karola must have been a wonderful nurse. When I first met her in Auschwitz she was about thirty-five years old.

She was not eager to reveal her intimate secrets. Always she seemed to be lost in thought. I knew very little about her. Her coolness was intimidating. I saw her often, since Karola worked on the hospital block. Her manner was unchanging: calm and quiet.

It was rumored in the camp that Karola had left two children with her sister—a thirteen-year-old daughter and five-year-old son. She very rarely spoke about them. Apparently she feared that the mere mention of them might have the power to bring them here to her. Rumor had it that Karola's sister had found a place outside the ghetto, among good gentile friends, and that there she took care of Karola's children.

I remember that hot summer day when Karola was informed that her sister, along with the children, was on the ramp in Auschwitz, waiting with the others for the arrival of the German doctor.

It was twelve o'clock. Dr. Koenig was in the clinic, looking over the sick. He was tall and skinny and gloomy. Even so, we preferred him to Dr. Mengele, who often talked to the sick like a benefactor. Suddenly the door of the infirmary opened and Karola burst in like a hurricane. She kneeled in the middle of the infirmary and stretched out her hands to Dr. Koenig in a beseeching way. She begged for the lives of her children. Orli, who had come into the infirmary with Karola, was standing next to her. Karola was lucky.

Mengele was not in the infirmary that day. If he had been there he would have sent her to the gas chamber along with the children, because the children could not live in the camp and they could not be sent to the gas chamber by themselves. It would not be humanitarian.

Koenig was taken aback for a moment, and Orli added hurriedly that Karola was a professional nurse and a very good worker.

Koenig said, "Come with me, then, and take your children!"

Orli went with Karola in order to help her get the children through the gate.

In the evening I went to the neighboring block where Karola lived. She was sitting with her children on the highest bed. Since the girl was tall and, like her mother, well-built, Karola had no trouble in adding three years to her recorded age. She was put down as sixteen on her registration card, and a number was tattooed on her arm. The age of little Zbyszek was difficult to cover up. He was five years old and small-framed. Slim, though tall, he had dark brown hair, bangs combed onto his forehead, and a dark complexion, all of which were brightened by beautiful blue-gray sparkling eyes. He sat cuddled up to his mother with fear in his eyes. He looked at that terrible world, at those sick lying in the beds around him, and he listened. His head was held at a tilt as though he was constantly listening and was ready to escape.

Karola's daughter Krysia had to start work as a *läufer* the next day. She started her adult life, if that is what you can call it, in Auschwitz. What was to be done with Zbyszek? With Orli's help she had smuggled him into the camp. Since he did not have a number he did not actually exist. Koenig knew about the boy, and the question was how would he behave? Would he appear one day and take Zbyszek to the gas chambers with the other children? The mercy of the German gods rode a fitful horse—that we knew very well.

Karola withered and aged. Zbyszek lay hidden on the top bunk when she was at work. You can imagine what Karola went through on every visit from Mengele or the other SS men on the block. She could never be certain that the boy would not become frightened and do something to draw attention to himself. Koenig never asked her about her children. He acted as if he knew nothing about the matter. There was no danger from that quarter.

A few months went by in this way. In the evening, after roll call, Zbyszek would crawl out of his hiding place, and Karola would go out to the front of the block with him. The boy had to walk and run a little.

Once I met them as they were going about their nightly exercise. It was the end of the summer and the chimneys were smoking without stop. Karola stood at an angle, looking around with the watchfulness of a hawk. Zbyszek ran around the block, taut as a string.

"You know, he is very frightened," Karola told me. "I had to tell him what would happen to him if the Germans see him. It is very important that he doesn't leave his bed during the day. He brought a book of poems with him. I taught him to read, and now he reads all day. He knows everything by heart. If I could get him some Polish books what a joy it would be for him."

Zbyszek came running toward us, fatigued, like any boy his age.

"You didn't see any Germans?" he asked with an air of sadness and tragedy, a vigilant look on his face.

The Germans did not visit us on Sundays. We felt freer than we usually did, and we would meet in the infirmary. That Sunday Karola came with her children. With her *läufer's* armband Krysia felt completely safe. Zbyszek recited some poems. He stood in the middle of the infirmary, quite handsome, and talked about a train sweating grease and oil. I looked at him and simply could not believe that there were people who desired his death. It was quiet in the infirmary, and Zbyszek's every word rang like the most beautiful music.

Suddenly the *sztubowa* ran into the infirmary from the next block.

"Mengele," she shouted.

I looked at Zbyszek. Till this day I see his pale face. He stood there as if turned to stone. We all jumped up. We hid Zbyszek under a mattress and made the bed over him. He did not protest. He did not say that he was uncomfortable or that he could not breathe. Karola ran to her block.

Half an hour later we pulled a barely breathing child from under the mattress.

"Has he gone for sure?" he asked. "Because I can lie here till
evening."

Zbyszek lived through Auschwitz. Although all the prisoners
knew about him, no one betrayed him to the Germans.

THE EXTERMINATION OF
THE MIDGETS

A transport arrived from Hungary late at night. Since there was no one in the infirmary at that late hour, Mengele ordered the SS men to break down the gate and take the family of midgets to the room located in the rear of the infirmary. Only the women were taken there as the men had already been taken to the men's camp.

Early that morning we arrived at the infirmary as usual, before roll call. In the infirmary we found three female midgets, two normal women who were married to midgets, and a three-year-old boy who was the son of a midget. In its entirety the family consisted of ten people. They had all been circus performers in Budapest.

The father of the family was a midget, and the mother was a tall, strong woman. She had borne only midgets: three daughters and three sons. The women had normal nicely shaped heads and curly hair. They spoke good German in a clear, bright voice. Their height, about fifty centimeters, did not bother them. Their short stature and their small feet and hands were the source of considerable attention, and the attention was not solely professional. "We have had proposals of marriage," they assured us and told us how certain men played with them as if they were dolls. One of the sons had married a normal woman, a pretty girl who had given birth to a normal boy in good physical condition.

"Is this really the son of that midget?" asked Mengele.

The other SS men were not stingy with jokes about that subject either.

Of the millions who came to Auschwitz, Mengele loved to single out those who had not been created "in God's image." I remember how he once brought a woman to our area who had two noses. Another time he brought a girl of about ten years of age who had the wool of a sheep on her head instead of hair. On another occasion, he brought a woman who had donkey ears. Now he had brought the midgets. Every day he asked for the "models" to be brought to the infirmary. He photographed them and examined them. In front of us he pretended that he was pursuing purely intellectual interests, but we knew that he was being driven by his personal sadism, gloating over the misfortunes of others, putting on display what he knew people would most like to hide. He would toy with his victims for a while and then kill them.

The three sisters had brought with them their tiny chairs and a little table. They arranged the miniature furniture in their room. The mother decorated the room very elegantly. The midgets had even brought powder and lipstick. They painted themselves and waited for the arrival of Mengele.

"How beautiful he is, how kind." They repeated it every minute. "How fortunate that he became our protector. How good of him to ask if we have everything."

They almost melted in adoration. They were accustomed to exposing themselves in public, and this was like another show for them. Only the young woman with the child was filled with anxiety. The boy was pretty, blond, calm, and sad.

"What do you think? What will he do with him?" the mother asked. "There are no children here. Will they kill him?"

What could we tell her? She and her child were in mortal danger. We knew it very well.

In the afternoon, Mengele came to the infirmary as usual. We all stood at attention, including the midgets. Next to them we looked like giants. He looked at them very closely. Then one of them stepped out of the row and fell at his boots. She was just about as tall as his boot. She hugged it with feeling and started to kiss it. "You are so kind, so gorgeous. God should reward you," she whispered, enraptured. He did not move for a minute, then he simply shook her off his boot. She fell. She lay there, tiny, spread out on the floor. "Now tell me how you lived with your midget." The old woman blushed so that the blood almost came pouring out of her.

"Speak!" screamed Mengele. "Later you will tell your story," he said to the young one. "You will tell me if the little one is the midget's son, or did you have him with somebody else?"

We all stood there like blocks of stone. The elderly woman was telling about her husband, that he was good and smart and that he earned a lot of money in the circus.

"Don't tell me about that, only about how you slept with him." Mengele was salivating.

The sweat poured down her face in big drops and fell on her clothes. She spoke, and he asked questions. I cannot repeat the conversation. It was grotesque, inhuman torture.

"Now you tell the story," he said to the young one.

She wanted to talk. Her mouth opened but there was no voice. She moved her lips like a fish. She pressed the child to herself.

"Is this his child?" he screamed.

She moved her head but she was unable to speak.

He left. The midgets crept away to their room, sad and subdued. Well, that's how the angel was. What would happen to them now? How would they live here? For a few days Mengele did not come to the infirmary, but we knew that he had not forgotten them, that he was looking for something. The orchestra came to the area, and we all went to listen to the music. The midgets went too. They sat on their little chairs, all dressed up and coquettish. The young woman with the child sat next to me. Everything looked so innocent and idyllic that I trembled with fear. I don't know why, but at such times I always waited for a blow. I listened for the footsteps of death, with whom we walked arm in arm. At that exact moment Marusia came running to take the child. Mengele had come to the infirmary to examine him.

"Examine him for what," shouted the mother. "He's not sick."

She went along with the child, grasping him tightly by the neck. Mengele threw her out of the infirmary. He remained alone with the boy. Marusia joined us, Mengele having ordered her to leave. We no longer heard the music. I watched the mother circling the infirmary like a wounded bird.

Every few minutes she came running back to us.

"What is he doing to my child?" She grabbed our hands and demanded an answer. We knew that at that moment the little boy was a guinea pig on whom an experiment was being performed to prove some pseudo theory of this murderer in a white apron. There was no force on earth that could have torn the child out of

Mengele's hands at that moment. Maybe death would free him from the torture of the experiments. Without blinking an eye, Mengele was inflicting physical agonies on a three-year-old child who had not the least understanding of what was happening.

Finally he left. We all rushed into the infirmary. The boy was lying on the table, still alive. Mancy wanted to see if he was all right, but the mother would not allow it. She grabbed the half-dead child and went into a mad frenzy of pain. She ran around the table. Not one drop of blood was left in his little face.

"He will die. He has to die," she said, choked with tears.

At night, the little one died. He never regained consciousness. In the small room, on the little table, lay the dead boy. Around him, like pillars of stone, stood the old lady, a large woman; the child's mother, slim and frail; the three midgets sat in miniature chairs. They did not cry. They were all frightened of the torturous death awaiting them. They sat that way until evening. Kwieta took the child and put the dead body with the other corpses that had been taken from the area on the *leichenauto.*

Now we lived in constant fear. We were waiting for Mengele to reach for the next victim for his experiments. A few days passed uneventfully. Mengele did not come to the infirmary. Koenig looked over the sick patients. An air of mourning filled the little room. Silence and sadness dominated.

One afternoon, *kapo* Bubi burst into the room. She was a German prisoner with a black triangle. We feared her as much as we feared the SS men. She used to come in often to flirt with Orli. She was a lesbian. We all knew about it and we were afraid of her, but we were also repelled by her flirtations. With great relish she described to us all the tragic occurrences in the camp. Today she came in happy and with a twinkle in her eye.

"Where are your midgets? Let them see who is lying near the wire," she said, laughing raucously. "Imagine," she continued, "the old midget wanted his wife. He was constantly making a nuisance of himself with everybody. He begged them to let him see his family. The *blokowy* and the *sztubowi* had to laugh at him. They told him, 'Okay, go ahead. You're so small that you can slip through the wires.' Would you believe it, he took them seriously, and this afternoon he started to sneak up to the wires. Everybody had a good show. I tell you, it was too bad you didn't see it. He looked around, but he couldn't see what the guard was doing. He couldn't see that high."

Bubi was laughing uncontrollably, as if she had just heard an unbearably funny joke, and at the same time she was watching us. She was waiting for us to join in the laughter.

"But you know, the guard wasn't one second late. When the midget got close enough to the wires the guard popped him. He never made it to his wife."

Bubi was bursting with happiness.

We left the infirmary. From a distance you could see the dead midget. His fellow prisoners were as much to blame for his misfortune as the SS man who actually put the bullet into him. That was the tragedy of Auschwitz.

very day deathly undernourished women and hundreds of mortally sick people came through the doors of the infirmary to which was attached a little cottage that housed the personnel who worked in the infirmary. Actually, it was not really a cottage but a little shack without windows. The total area of the shack was about two by six meters. Inside there were two three-decker beds and a small table. We thought that it was the most wonderful habitation in the world. It was our corner, different from the terrible barracks.

One sunny day we received a notice that hit us like a clap of thunder. It was a summer evening in 1944 when Orli brought us the news that we would have to move out of our little shack because Mengele had decided to create a ward for mentally disturbed women. At night we removed our meager possessions. The next morning we waited for the patients. The whole affair looked very suspicious to me. It was difficult to understand why Mengele would create a ward for the mentally sick in the infirmary. Until now there had been no such ward. We had a feeling that Mengele must have a new trick up his sleeve.

First thing in the morning they brought the first patient. Her name was Natasha. The *blokowa* brought her in.

"She has to stay here with you in the infirmary," the *blokowa* said and left.

Before me stood a young girl, straight as a tree, with a gloomy, rebellious face. She was nineteen years old and from Leningrad. She would not tell us anything else. Our Jewish doctors were not invited to examine her, since their findings were set at no value. Natasha immediately took an upper bunk. She lay there quietly, saying nothing, but when we brought her some soup she came to life, and a big smile brightened up her face. She ate while she continued to lie there without saying a word.

The same afternoon, five new patients were brought in, including two German, one Dutch, and two French women. They were all very young and very sad. At first we were afraid of them. We imagined that they would cause trouble, maybe have fits. Perhaps we would have to use physical force to subdue them. We had no experience in handling such cases. But the new patients lay quietly in their beds, or else they sat bent over on the edge of the bed.

I remember that I made several attempts to talk to them, but my words did not reach them. That same day, just before roll call, a few more women were brought in. By this time a few of the beds were being shared by two women. A couple of mornings later we prepared the infirmary to receive a visit from Dr. Mengele. We knew that he would come to examine the new "ward." That morning, as we were admitting the sick to the hospital, we did not accept the very sick ones. We sent them back to the blocks. We knew that if he started looking at them he would certainly send them to the ovens. It was with heavy hearts that we sent those women away to do heavy labor, women who were barely alive, with swollen legs and terrible sores all over their bodies. But we well knew the monster in the white coat who had the face of a Romeo. He would assign them to the gas and then would say to us, "You see yourselves that these women are not strong enough to live. Why should they suffer? I am sending them to the gas for their own good."

Mengele arrived about twelve o'clock.

"Achtung," shouted Marusia.

The selection of the sick and the signing of the cards started. Everything was going smoothly, without a hitch. All of a sudden, from the next room, we heard a loud, happy voice calling,

"Hey, you! Doctor! Maybe you can come in and see us."

It was Natasha calling to Mengele; she was speaking to him in beautiful German, her voice radiant with happiness.

"What are you afraid of, coward, you who can murder women and children? Come here. We will discuss your Hitler's crimes. Maybe you want to discuss Stalingrad, where you are dying like mad dogs."

We turned to stone. Every one of us pretended to be very busy. We were afraid to look in his direction. We knew that in a minute something terrible would happen. Natasha's ringing, violent voice floated in from the other room.

"You will all die in Russia, the way Napoleon did. You are afraid to come to me. You don't want to listen to the truth, you specialist of the gas chambers."

Suddenly we saw Mengele get up and go into the other room. I waited for a shot and automatically covered my ears with my fists.

"Come, sit next to us. We will have a chat."

Mengele did not say a thing. Only the voice of Natasha could be heard.

"Hitler, that human garbage, destroyed Germany. All the nations will hate you through the ages. You will see. Even if you live through the war, you will have to hide from human revenge like a worm."

We stood there completely motionless, as though hypnotized. Natasha started to sing. What a wonderful voice she had.

She finished the interview with an abrupt, "Get out of here. I can't stand to look at your shiny mug any more."

Mengele got up and left without a word. Only after he had crossed the threshold of the infirmary and had looked at our pale faces did he shout out the order to dress all the sick, because the orderly would come to pick them up after lunch.

"The Russian is to stay here," he added in closing.

We knew what that meant. The orderly would give them an injection of phenol, and in the evening the *leichenauto* would take them to the gas chambers. Natasha had to remain here. Why? Maybe he was preparing a more agonizing death for her.

The next day they brought a new batch of women. They, too, were sad and silent. About lunch time Mengele came in again.

"Come here, hero of the gas chambers," Natasha called again. "We will discuss your death. If you wish, I will tell you how you're going to die."

With wonder we watched him approach Natasha. For an hour she carried on a tirade against Hitler. She sang Russia's praises. Mengele sat on the chair with his head hung low on his chest.

I remember looking at him and not believing my own eyes. What was going on here? What was drawing that predator to his prey? To this very day I cannot understand what secret was lurking behind his behavior. Maybe it was just one more aberration.

Perhaps the flagellation he received from Natasha's tongue gave him some sort of satisfaction.

Every day the sanitation worker took the sick for the *szpryce* (injection). That was their term for murder by phenol in Auschwitz. Every day Mengele came to listen to Natasha's speeches. One evening I decided to have a talk with Natasha. I told her everything about myself, waiting for her to get up enough confidence so that she would be willing to tell me about her life. I was not mistaken.

Natasha had been a student. Her parents had been professors of German. It was from them that she had learned such elegant German. After that conversation I was certain that Natasha was not mentally ill and that she was feigning mental illness in order to be able to get away with telling the Germans exactly how she felt about them.

"But dear Natasha," I screamed with anguish, "do you know what they do to mentally ill people? They don't heal but kill."

"I know," said Natasha. "But I don't want to live in this rotten world."

The next day Dr. Koenig came for the inspection instead of Mengele. We closed the door to the little room. Maybe we could hide the sick from him.

"Hey, you, Doctor of death," Natasha shouted in a loud voice. "Come here, we will discuss your Hitler."

Koenig shuddered. He pushed open the door and went into the little room. The room was almost completely dark. On the beds sat the huddled figures.

"What, you're afraid to come in, you Hitler's coward?"

Then there was a shot. All the sick screamed at the same time, with a terrible, hollow voice.

When we reached Natasha she was already dead.

s it possible to put a price on life? I do not mean somebody else's life but one's own. Can a definite price be set on life, or is it priceless? That is, does life have a value beyond any price? If so, then it is all right knowingly to send other people to be gassed, those prisoners who had been deprived by the almighty Germans of the right to live. Moreover, when death is inevitable is there any point in fighting for life? Is there really such a thing as a meaningful death? Is it better for a human being to face death, knowing that he is about to die, or is it better when death comes upon him suddenly, snuffing him out before he realizes what is happening?

In Auschwitz, a place where death was palpable, where the air was filled with death groans, those questions flowed through our minds continuously. For us these were not merely academic questions. The way you answered these questions determined the way you behaved toward other people, including those who were condemned to death. Those who asserted, "I want to live at any price," would put even their own parents into the car that was going to the crematorium. On the other hand, parents who wanted to live at any price put their small children into valises and then cast the valises aside. Those who asserted, "My life is priceless," dragged out prisoners who were hiding during the selection so that they themselves would be able to escape the danger.

It seems odd, but in Auschwitz everybody wanted to live. Suicides were very rare. In this terrible world there was room for hope and dreams. The most beautiful images of life after the war shimmered in the mind's eye. We imagined that after the war people would be richer for the experience and would create a paradise on earth, without wars and without persecution. Is it any wonder that everyone wanted to see the defeat of Germany and the world that would come into being after that took place? The real challenge was to find the will to overcome the animal instinct of survival at all cost, as reflected in the cynical proverb "Better a living dog than a dead lion," and to avoid being sucked into the pervasive bestiality.

Is it better for a human being to know that he is about to die? I remember living through a bombing while I was in the forest near Slonim. I was so totally exhausted after my escape from Bialystok that I fell asleep in the midst of danger. Every time a bomb exploded I would wake up and say to myself, "Don't sleep. You will not even know when death comes." In Auschwitz I sometimes wondered whether this might not be the significance of the nightly prayer: "Grant me light, oh Lord, lest I sleep the sleep of death." The meaning of that prayer to the Lord is to protect one from unexpected death during the watches of the night so that a human being may be conscious and bid farewell to life.

Magda, a small Slovak who worked with us in the infirmary, tried to convince us that she experienced her greatest suffering when she watched people going to the gas chambers without knowing what was awaiting them.

"Let them at least know where they are going. Every human being has the right to a conscious death," said Magda.

"What benefit will accrue to them from knowing where they are going?" we answered. "They will only suffer longer."

"Let them suffer, but let them die like human beings. Our responsibility is to tell them about it."

t was fall 1944. On that cloudy day the roll call dragged on endlessly. Every few minutes we would look through the wires only to see columns of tired women. *Rapportführer* Taube, who had taken over the roll call that day, was running from one block to the other, checking and counting. The SS women ran in his footsteps, terribly nervous. Apparently not knowing what else to do, the *blokowe* kept calling out, "Achtung!" The women braced themselves for the worst. Later, all the *blokowe* were called to the *rapportführer* and issued some sort of order. They quickly returned to their blocks and, with the clerks, wrote down the numbers of the women who were standing in columns. Every prisoner feared that most of all.

"Why are they writing down the numbers?" we wondered. "Are all the prisoners designated for the gas?" In Auschwitz you could expect the worst every minute. Here you walked arm in arm with death.

Having written down the numbers, the *blokowe* ran to give them to Taube. Right after that the sirens started wailing. For us the wail of the sirens was the most beautiful music we could hear in the camp, because the sirens sounded only for two reasons: when a prisoner escaped or when an "enemy" plane was spotted overhead. The sound of the sirens in this instance meant that a prisoner had escaped. No sooner had the roll call ended than the whole contingent of SS men and their dogs started on the hunt.

The next day we discovered exactly who had escaped. Mala, a Jewess from Belgium who worked as a *läufer* in the camp, had escaped from the women's section. Her boyfriend, who was a Polish political prisoner, had escaped from the men's section. For a few days the fugitives remained at large. Among the women in our area there was a holiday atmosphere. Since Mala was a member of the anti-Fascist movement, we figured that, if she escaped, she would spread the news of what was happening in this Hell. Now, every time we met we would greet each other with the same questions: "How is it with Mala? Is she still free?" What pleasure her escape gave us! I remember waking up at night, watching the rats running around near the oven, and thinking of Mala. What was she doing right now? How happy she must be now that she had torn herself away from this Hell and saw free people all around her.

Everyone in the camp knew Mala. She had been a *läufer* for several years. She was fluent in several languages, and I found her particularly pleasant because she spoke Polish very well. She told me that her parents had emigrated from Poland to Belgium after World War I, and since they always spoke Polish to each other she had learned to speak their native language. In the camp Mala was a kind of *überläufer*, if that is the word for it. She had earned the respect of the other *läufers*. They listened to her and believed her. She was willing to undertake even the riskiest tasks, and she always brought them off.

When I met Mala in January 1944 she was twenty years old. She was a tall girl, very agile, with long, blond hair and a pleasant face. She was courageous almost to the point of madness. There was no assignment too difficult for her to carry out. She was able to pull out of the office file identity cards of women who were designated to be gassed and replace them with the cards of women who had died long ago. With her skill and daring, she had managed to save the lives of many women. She knew about everything that was being planned in the camp. She brought us news about new transports and about plans for deportations. She listened to the radio and brought us news about the situation at the front. Sometimes she even managed to steal a German newspaper for us.

I remember how she came bursting in with the joyous news about the capture of Lublin by the Russian and Polish armies. She was always happy and had a sunny disposition. The word in Auschwitz was that it was her radiant spirit that had kindled her great love for Tadeusz. I never discussed the subject with her, but I always believed that her great pride, courage, and belief in people were all the result of her grand passion.

Now Mala and Tadeusz were together and free. We knew that the Germans would not give up the search easily. If they did not find them in the camp area they would look for them in the cities.

They must not do anything careless. Their struggle for life and freedom was not over yet.

At the end of October, three weeks after their escape, we were informed that Mala and her boyfriend were once again in the bunkers of Auschwitz. They were caught in Katowice, where they were terribly beaten and then brought back to the camp. The prisoners who brought us the laundry told us that they had been put in the bunkers and that the SS men were trying to pry out of them how they had managed to escape and the names of those to whom they may have revealed the secrets of Auschwitz. It was not difficult for the SS to figure out that they could not have escaped without help and that there must be some organization operating in the camp. They wanted Mala and her boyfriend to give them the names of those who had helped them and of those who belonged to the organization. They were taken out for interrogation a few times a day, and each time they were beaten inhumanly. Would they be able to stand the punishment? Would they break down?

The whole camp was talking about it. This pair became a fascinating symbol for all of the inmates. Their love affair, their courageous flight, and now their torment had all the elements of the tragedy of Romeo and Juliet, set in Auschwitz. Like the Greek heroes in the face of unyielding fate, we were completely helpless to do anything about the death that surely awaited them. We did not know, yet, just what kind of bizarre execution the SS were cooking up for them, but we did know that anyone who tried to help them would also surely die with them.

Day to day we waited for the finale of the tragedy to take its course. It was a cold and misty night. The *komando* was returning from work to the camp. Roll call usually took place right there in front of the blocks, and only after that would the women come to the infirmary to have their wounds dressed. This October night it was different. The *komando* did not go to the blocks. They crowded everybody close to the gate, dividing field "A" from field "B." There they set up a mock tribunal. At the last moment a gallows was erected. They ordered the women to each side of the gate. The *blokowe* and *sztubowe* were already there. Then came

Ilse Koch, commander of the camp, accompanied by several SS men.

We stood in the doorway of the infirmary waiting for the heroine of the bloody celebration. We knew who was going to be hung. We did not have to wait long. Mala walked slowly, erect, escorted by two SS men, one on either side. In front of the trio walked another prisoner, clearing a path for them. "Mala, Mala"—a whisper issued from a thousand lips like a single sigh. She smiled faintly. "Mala, Mala," I whispered in despair. Slowly she came closer and closer to the gate, drawing nearer to death with each step. She stood at the elevation next to the commander of the camp. Ilse came forward and started to make a speech.

This was the first time that the death of a prisoner had been set up in so ceremonial a fashion. Mala, standing behind the commander, slowly pulled a razor out of concealment. She started to cut her veins. All the SS men were so busy staring at Ilse, so engrossed in her words, that they did not see Mala cut the veins on one hand and then, with bloody palm, start to cut the veins in the second arm. The prisoners gave her away. One enormous sigh was heaved from their collective breasts. In a fairy tale, where good always triumphs, that sigh should have destroyed the platforms that Ilse Koch and the SS men were standing on.

Ilse stopped the speech, turned around quickly, and saw the victim who, at the last moment of her life, dared to defy Ilse's will. She pounced on Mala in an attempt to tear the razor out of her hand. Mala measured out a blow on Ilse's huge cheek, leaving the bloody trace of her palm on Ilse's face. The SS men disarmed Mala, and the *blokowe* chased the women back to the blocks. Ilse Koch never got to finish her speech.

Mala was not hanged. The SS men brought her staggering to the infirmary. She slowly sank to the floor, blood gushing from her veins. Instinctively, the girls moved in her direction. They wanted to save her. What for? So that she could die a second death? She was lying on the floor in a puddle of blood, almost unconscious.

They would not let her die peacefully in the infirmary. A minute later an SS man came running with a prisoner from the *sonderkomando* who was pushing a wheelbarrow. They threw Mala into the wheelbarrow and quickly rushed off toward the crematorium. Her bloody hands were dangling over the sides of the wheelbarrow, and her blonde head did not fit in the wagon. That was the last time I saw Mala.

The prisoners told us later that when they brought Mala through the gate dividing the men's camp from the women's camp, the corpse of Tadeusz was hanging on the gate. "Goodbye, my love," whispered Mala with dying lips. Ilse wanted Mala to be thrown into the oven alive. That was to be her revenge for the aborted ceremony and for the slap that Mala had delivered in front of all the women. But the SS man who worked in the crematorium did not carry out her orders. He shot Mala with his own hands and then threw her body into the oven.

That is how Mala and Tadeusz died. Unfortunately, I do not remember their last names. The lovers of Auschwitz. Beautiful, brave, tragic in their loving and their dying. Their love and death could become the theme of a tragedy written in a barbarous age.

THE DANCE OF THE RABBIS

here came a day when Magda was ready to stand in front of the infirmary and shout at the top of her voice, "People, don't let them deceive you. You are on the way to die in the gas chambers!"

That day a transport arrived in the late afternoon. We heard the noise of the train and the whistles of the SS men. We closed the gate, but through a crack we watched what was happening on the ramp. We had become accustomed to watching the goings on, because the trains stopped in front of the infirmary. It was a hot, stuffy summer day. A thick stench hung in the air. The people were leaving the wagons. Mengele, as usual, was performing the selections. Out of one of the wagons came a group of about a hundred rabbis. They were all dressed in long, black, satin coats and black hats, and some of them were even wearing fur caps in spite of the intense heat. All of them were elderly and they all had long, white beards. Where did they get them all? How did they manage to round up that many rabbis in a single transport? Since the train came from Hungary, these must have been Hungarian rabbis.

Mengele shunted them off to the side. We guessed instantly that they were trying to figure out something special for them. Between the tracks and the infirmary was an empty wasteland full of holes and craters. This barren landscape was dotted with stones, refuse, wires, broken desks. Everything was flung there helter skelter. The SS men herded the rabbis into this barren area. They were squeezed closely together, fearful and troubled. We could not hear Mengele's orders, but we saw the tightly packed rabbis scatter, forming a huge circle that started moving on the uneven terrain in some sort of a macabre dance. Some of them tripped and fell, breaking the rhythm of the other dancing rabbis. Then you could hear the hum of the whip, and one of the old men would get to his feet and resume dancing.

Apparently Mengele issued a new command, because they now lifted their eyes and arms to heaven. They kept on dancing. Mengele must have demanded a new Jewish dance. They shrugged their shoulders as though demanding an answer of the invisible God who, in spite of the fact that they had served him so loyally, had now abandoned them.

"Singen!" we heard Mengele scream.

Suddenly a beautiful melody swelled through the camp, a hymn to the Lord. It was the *Kol Nidrei* prayer, which is sung by Jews in the synagogue on the evening preceding *Yom Kippur.* They circled round the barren wasteland, singing their plaintive, yearning melody to God. Now they were no longer singing in obedience to Mengele's orders. They now chanted their defiance before the SS men who were herding their bodies to the gas chambers. In spite of their degradation and suffering they still believed in the mission of the Jewish people. Disappearing behind the gates of the gas chambers they cried out,

"Hear, oh, Israel. God is with us. God is One."

Near the trains, thousands of people who had come with the rabbis looked on fearfully and passively. Then, little Magda, a girl of eighteen, bolted to the gate of the infirmary and started to open it.

"What are you doing? Do you want them to shoot us?" we yelled excitedly.

"I'm going outside by myself to tell these people that they're going to the gas chambers, just like the rabbis. Let them yell. Let the Germans chase them. Let them die while they are running," Magda shouted.

"But those people won't believe your words. The SS men will shoot you before the people can get the information. They won't believe you because they want to live. Your sacrifice will be useless."

We stood near the gate, keeping a tight hold on Magda, that light-haired maiden with the face of the Madonna. After all, was it fair to take all hope from those people for the short time that divided them from death? One was speaking of an honorable death. But was death so dishonorable in this situation in which a fight was impossible? That is how we thought at the time. What is the case, really? It is hard to find the right answer.

REVENGE OF A DANCER

During the summer of 1944 the transports used to arrive at Auschwitz at night as well as in the daytime. We often woke up because of the shouting of the SS men, the barking of dogs, the whistling of trainmen, the stamping of hundreds of feet, and the cries of desperation in different languages. At night the atrocities combined with our sleeplessness to give us a very vivid sense of existing in a factory of death. And yet, it all appeared unreal.

This particular July night it was the shouting of the SS men and the barking of the dogs that awakened me. I was lying on my narrow mattress thinking of those unfamiliar people going on their last trip. Suddenly the air was shattered by a series of shots, and then you could hear the sound of someone running. Then more shots, more shouts, and lamentations. It lasted a long time, almost the whole of a short summer night. Something was going on at the train station. Someone had fouled up an order given by the Germans.

According to my usual custom, I went to the infirmary before roll call, not yet dressed. Since there was running water in the infirmary it was possible for me to wash up. At the gate of the infirmary I met Marusia.

"Come quickly to the infirmary," she said. "We have to figure what we should do."

Except for the two of us, everybody was already in the infirmary. There was a young girl wearing Mancy's sweater. She sat there hunched over, so frightened that she did not know what she was saying. We knew we had to get all the information immediately in order to help her. She spoke French and a little German. Marusia ran to get Masha, who was French, in the hope that the girl would trust her more than she trusted us and would tell us how she managed to get here so early in the morning with practically no clothes on.

When Marusia had arrived that morning she found the girl, who had barely managed to cover herself with a rag that had been glued to the wall of the barrack. She took the shivering girl inside and gave her Mancy's sweater but made no attempt to question her. In this condition the girl was unable to speak. When she saw Masha she softened up, and this is what we heard.

"We arrived at Auschwitz last night. We traveled in standard Pullman cars. The transport consisted of five hundred people: men, women, and children. We were told that we were being taken east to work. They treated us well and fed us. As we were on our way to Poland, strangers shouted to us that we were on our way to death and that we should run away. We didn't believe such 'nonsense.' Why should we run away? We were going to work and we would all be in one place. As soon as we crossed the Polish border, the leaders of the convoy started treating us more brutally.

"When we reached Auschwitz there was nobody at the station. It seems that nobody expected us at that hour. It was dark and quiet. In my compartment there were women with children and a young dancer from Paris. She was an unusually beautiful woman, very pleasant and courteous. She helped the mothers keep the children amused. Since it was very hot, we all wore bathing suits. The dancer was wearing a two-piece suit. We were all very tired from the long trip, so we dozed as we waited to leave the cars.

"We were awakened by boots with spurs and the barking of dogs. We started to get dressed and to get our luggage together, as is usually done when a train pulls into a station. All of a sudden the door of our compartment opened with a loud noise, and a sleepy SS man told us to strip naked and to come out to the station, leaving all our clothes and baggage behind in the cars.

" 'What do you mean? You want us to go out to the station naked?' we asked, not believing what we had heard.

"When we stood there, undecided, he started hitting us with the rifle butt.

" 'Schneller, Schneller,' they shouted from all sides.

"We started to undress. Later, the SS men burst into the compartments with dogs and chased us outside. We were not allowed to stand for a minute. We had to go forward completely naked: men, women, and children. The dancer, still in her bathing suit, was walking next to me. She was the only one who did not get undressed. An SS man, apparently the commandant of the guards, approached her. 'Beautiful girl, take off your suit,' he said quietly, coming closer and closer to her. Then, all of a sudden, with a rapid movement, she grabbed the pistol out of his holster and shot straight at him. After that, she took three steps backward and shot at the SS men who were running all over the place. She saved the last bullet for herself. She fell to the ground. The panic was extraordinary. There was shooting and yelling from every direction. We couldn't run away because we were naked and we didn't know the camp. I stood next to the heroic, dead girl not knowing what to do next. Suddenly, I felt somebody grab my hand and throw a dress in my direction. Then he pulled me by the hand and dragged me behind some gate, finally bringing me here. It was a German soldier. He left without a word."

This was the story of the young French girl. We listened to the story as if we were hearing the most beautiful music.

"That's how you're supposed to die," said Magda.

We did not discuss the subject further. That day a French girl died in the camp. Our arrival from the night transport was given her number and her name. Who was the German soldier who had saved a young Jewish girl's life? We never found out.

THE VERDICT

n October 1944 the whole hospital was moved to camp "C," the old gypsy camp. That is when I met Mrs. Helena. She had been doing the same job I was doing, except that she was a clerk in the infirmary for non-Jewish prisoners. In the new block, the separate infirmaries were liquidated and combined into one. The new infirmary was located in a separate barrack. In addition to the reception room there was a beautiful room containing three bunk beds. Five of the beds were occupied by the workers in the infirmary: Helena and I, the clerks; Mancy and Frieda, the two doctors; and nurse Marusia. The sixth bed was taken by Kwieta, who worked in the *leichenkomando*.

Mrs. Helena stuck out oddly in our group of five. Perhaps because she was older than we were, we felt very inhibited in her presence. She maintained a constant silence and seemed always to be steeped in her own thoughts. She lived her own life and said nothing to anyone. We did not even know how she had gotten to Auschwitz. She was slim, light-haired, and had an inscrutable face. She did not take part in our discussions, and she never judged anybody. She eavesdropped on our gossiping and seemed to be saying, "I would like to see how you would behave in a similar situation."

One evening, while we were discussing conscious and unconscious death, we were surprised to hear Helena break heatedly into our discussion:

"Listen to the story I am going to tell you about the death of 156 girls from Krakow, and then you can tell me what you think of the way I behaved." We all stopped talking, and complete silence descended on our cell.

"We were just finishing receiving the sick," Mrs. Helena started quietly. "While Mengele was looking over the women who had been admitted to the area, we had but one thought in our minds: we hoped he would leave soon. I remember that it was a scorching July day. The atmosphere in the infirmary was almost unbearable. The last sick woman moved through the line, passing in front of the German doctor. We heaved a sigh of relief. Mengele got up slowly, buttoned his uniform, stood facing me, and said: 'At fifteen hours the *leichenauto* will come; I will come at fourteen hours.' We looked at one another in dumb amazement. Why the *leichenauto* at fifteen hours? Usually, the car came to pick up the dead after darkness had fallen. What was Mengele planning to do here at fourteen hours? We couldn't speak. We were all sure that the *leichenauto* was coming for us, to take us to the crematorium. We had to start cleaning up, but you can believe that everything kept dropping out of our hands, and that the hours dragged on without end. It's not easy to wait for the worst. After all, I don't have to tell you about that.

"At thirteen hours two young girls came to the infirmary, Poles from Krakow. They told us that the *blokowa* had ordered them to report here because they had to leave for work in Germany and Mengele was going to examine them. I was so frightened by what I heard that I almost fainted. 'Is it only you the *blokowa* sent?' I asked in a quivering voice.

" 'Not just us,' they answered. 'There will be a lot more of us here. The rest will be coming soon. We came in first because we are in a hurry to join the transport that is leaving Auschwitz.'

"Quite a large number of women were now gathering in front of the infirmary, most of them young. They were happy to be leaving Auschwitz. They were talking loudly, laughing, never dreaming that they had been horribly deceived and that the *leichenauto* was coming for them in about an hour. For us it was all clear; those Poles were condemned to death, and the sentence was going to be carried out in the infirmary. 'What to do?' I thought feverishly. Maybe I should tell them why they had been summoned here. Perhaps I should shout it out to them: 'Calm down! Don't laugh. You are living corpses, and in a few hours nothing will be left of you but ashes!' Then what? Then we attendants would go to the gas chambers and the women would die anyway. The women might run and scatter all over the camp, but in the end they would get caught. Their numbers have been recorded. There is no place for them to run.

"Believe me, we quietly took counsel, trying to decide what to do. We didn't tell them the terrible truth, not out of fear for our own lives, but because we truly did not know what would be the least painful way for the young women to die. Now they didn't know anything, they were carefree, and death would be upon them before they knew it. If we told them what was in store for them, then a struggle for life would ensue. In their attempt to run from death they would find only loneliness, because their friends, seeking to preserve their own lives, would refuse to help them. There were more than 150 women in front of the infirmary. They stood in rows of five, as at roll call, and waited for the doctor to examine them. Still, we did not know what to do. All our reasoning told us to say nothing. Today I know that it was fear for our own lives that made us reason this way, that induced us to believe that sudden, unexpected death is preferable to a death that makes itself known to your full and open consciousness.

"Precisely at fourteen hours, Mengele arrived, accompanied by an orderly named Kler. He looked at the lines of women standing there and then at us in such a way as to make us partners in the crimes that he was about to commit. At that moment I knew that we had made a mistake in not telling the young women what was awaiting them. Whether dying is supposed to be easy or difficult, I suppose every individual has to decide for herself. But it was our duty to inform the young women what awaited them.

" 'Bring them in for a checkup,' shouted Mengele. The first girl walked in, the one who was in a hurry to leave Auschwitz. She stood in front of me; I did not say anything. By filling out her hospital card, I was taking part in this deception that was making it easy for Mengele to execute his victim. She walked in without suspecting anything. Then I heard the crashing sound of a falling body; later, the second; then the third, the tenth, the twentieth. Always the same: the card, the squeaking of the door, the crash of a falling body. The corpses were thrown out into the waiting room, which was located behind the reception room. An SS man with a dog kept order in front of the infirmary. Calm and trusting, the women kept going in. I lowered my head so they wouldn't see my face. All I would see each time was a hand stretched out to receive a card. I really did not understand why they were so calm. Weren't they surprised not to see the other women coming out of the infirmary after they had been examined? I looked for some sign of anxiety in those stretched out hands, but to no avail. I had given out about a hundred cards when it started.

"One of the girls asked the SS man why the other women weren't coming out after having been examined. Instead of answering her he hit her over the head with his rifle butt. Then I heard one of the girls yell, 'We are not going in there. They will give us an injection of phenol.' A terrible outcry started. The girls really refused to enter the infirmary. When one of them tried to run away the SS man shot her. At the sound of a shot a whole troop of SS men and dogs ran in. The young women were completely surrounded. Each girl, having first been beaten, was dragged screaming, by two SS men, into the presence of Mengele. I didn't give out any more cards. It was no longer necessary.

"I jumped up from my seat and hid in a corner of the infirmary. The women did not want to die. They tore themselves out of the grip of the SS men and started to run away. Then the dogs were set on them. Their deaths were completely different from the deaths of the first batch of women who went to their deaths unknowing. Who knows which death was more difficult, but the first group seemed to die more peacefully.

"At fifteen hours the *leichenauto* showed up, and an hour later the entire operation was completed. Up to the very last minute we were not certain that Mengele was not going to send us, the witnesses of that bloody happening, to the gas. Mengele left, calm, and with a smile he put down the sick card he had been holding. 'Herzanfall [heart attack],' he said."

Mrs. Helena finished her terrible tale. We did not utter a word. After a long pause she resumed: "I still don't know whether we should have told the women about the death that was waiting for them. What do you think?"

None of us said anything.

A cold, penetrating rain had been falling for a few days. Such rains were not unusual in Auschwitz. I opened the gate of the infirmary very quietly so as not to disturb the performance and listened. "Plop, plop,"—the drops continued falling without a stop. Outside it was dark and quiet. The lights on the ramp of the station were out. It had been a few days since the last trainload of victims had arrived at Auschwitz. Perhaps, I thought, they would not bring any more victims here.

I sat down in the corner to watch the performance. It was Sunday. Since everything was at peace this day, Irena had organized a cultural evening in the infirmary. She had planned an evening of dancing—without men, of course. But then, it is possible to dance without men, too.

Irena was an actress. Although she was originally from Poland, she had lived in Paris some fourteen years before being shipped to Auschwitz. She was tall, strong, and straight. I remember that when I first met her it was hard for me to believe that she was an actress. Looking at her, you would absolutely never guess that she was an actress. The girls who knew her swore that once she got on the stage she changed so completely that you would never recognize her. She was particularly wonderful, they said, as a character actress.

In Auschwitz we often organized such friendly get-togethers. I remember that for the first few months of my stay here those get-togethers struck me as being indecent. How was it possible that we could sing while the sky above was red with the flames of the crematoria.

"How can you joke, dance, and tell stories," I asked, "when we are enveloped in a sea of suffering, pain, and tears?"

"You will get used to it. Then you will understand." So said the old prisoners.

One evening, as I was returning from the infirmary to the barracks for the night, I bumped into a group of girls from the *lei-*

chenkomando, whose job it was to load the dead into the trucks. One of them stood near a pile of corpses, the second near the truck, the third on a small stool, and the fourth on the platform of the truck. They were handing the dead to each other any old way: grabbing the corpse by the leg, or the arm, or the hair, and then swinging it onto the platform. I noted their indifference to the dead and tried to imagine what kind of women they had been a few years ago, when they loved and were loved in a world of normality. Every few minutes I could hear a sound—the thump of falling flesh and the cries of the women: "Hurry up. Why are you dawdling?"

One of the women started singing a song and immediately the rest of them joined in: "For a cup of flour, he kissed for an hour."

They sang to the melody of a German march. I descended on them, half choking:

"How can you sing a merry song in front of those skeletons?" I called out resentfully.

They looked at me in bewilderment, without the foggiest notion of what I was talking about.

"You'll get used to it," one of them said. Then, after a moment's silence, she added: "If you don't get used to it you'll drop dead."

I got used to it. After eight months in Auschwitz, I could look at the dead with indifference. When a corpse was lying across my path I did not go around it any more, I simply stepped over it, as if I were merely stepping over a piece of wood. I sang along with the others, and I laughed when I heard a good joke. I even told jokes myself. I even got used to the rats warming themselves in front of the stove like cats. I had imbibed all of the terrors of Auschwitz and lived. Then I really understood that my ability to adapt to just about anything was a most useful talent. Was this good or bad? It was difficult for me to know.

High on the ceiling a small light bulb was burning; we were sitting around, scattered all over the room. Some were sitting on the table, some were sitting on the floor. Marusia and Kwieta and all of the other Czechs were singing a beautiful youth song about those who "defy the wind." The words of the song said that only by swimming against the current could the strong achieve satisfaction. The French girls were singing French songs about Paris. I specialized in Russian songs. I sang without thinking about the red sky. Somebody recited a poem. Then, in hushed tones, we sang a prison hymn in German. The conductor of the orchestra, a Hungarian woman, was the main attraction. She had come to the camp with her violin; now she started playing Hungarian and gypsy melodies. We were sitting around, listening, as if bewitched. Suddenly the door of the infirmary opened with a loud crash, and there stood Hitler: moustache, hair, and a haughty, stupid expression. We all jumped up from our places, and Marusia even yelled "Achtung!" Hitler walked in with a long stride and an outstretched hand and kneeled in front of me. He set his hands beseechingly and whispered, "Maybe you would like to change places with me."

We all burst into joyous laughter. It was Irena. She was mocking my assertion that we had it better than Hitler because we had more of a chance of living through the war. Hitler would certainly not live through the war, but we might. She got up. We could not get over her impersonation. With the help of black shoe polish she had changed her face beyond recognition.

Now the girls started dancing to the accompaniment of the violin. Orli was standing next to me, pale and agitated.

"Has something happened?" I asked.

"Walk outside unobtrusively," Orli said, "so that nobody will notice."

We left the infirmary. It was raining without letup. The ramp was lighted up. The SS men were standing in front of the cars. We had been feeling happy because the transports were not arriving. Now the unloading of the people was starting again, but quietly, without the usual screaming. Nude men came out, so skinny that it was difficult to believe that those people were moving on their own power. They were, indeed, moving skeletons.

"Those are Russian prisoners," Orli whispered. "They were working someplace, and now, since they are incapable of working any more, they are being sent to the gas chambers."

They walked slowly under the cold rain. Some of them were swaying. They all went to the gas chambers. The lights on the station went out, the empty cars left, and we just stood there, outside.

"Let's not tell the girls anything. Let's not spoil their fun," Orli said quietly. We did not return to the infirmary. To sing and joke now was beyond our strength. After all, you could not get used to everything.

oward the end of 1944 Russian planes used to fly over Auschwitz more frequently, and the wailing of the air-raid sirens could be heard not only at night but also during the day. I remember especially one alarm that sounded at noon time. A young SS man came to hide in our infirmary, a little embarrassed by the fact that he was seeking safety among us, "because," as he explained it, "the Russians won't drop any bombs on you." He was frightened to death, but we had to hide the joy we felt to hear the Russians bombing. That day a few women who had been working outside the camp perished during the attack. In the evening the returning *komando* brought their corpses with them.

In October that year the women's camp was moved to the former gypsy camp. The infirmary was located in a large barrack, with a large comfortable furnished room in the back for us. Instead of Magda there was now a young Russian girl who did the cleaning. She was bright and happy. The German doctors did not bother much with us. We felt the taste of freedom, and maybe the taste of death.

Marusia, Mancy, Kwieta, and Helena received packages from the free side, so we did not lack for food. Sometimes our friends came to visit us. They brought us linen, bandages, and sometimes they would sit with us for a few hours in our room. The SS men who came with them did not bother us. We started to see the future in rosy colors.

One afternoon toward the end of November 1944, after checking the sick into the hospital, we were sitting around in our room eating lunch. Completely unexpectedly, Mengele came to the infirmary. We became very frightened when we saw him, since he was an ill wind that never blew any good and since we were totally unprepared for his visit.

"Women from the new transport will be brought here very soon. Receive all of them into the area, and keep them waiting in the infirmary until I get here to take a look at them. I'll be back in a few hours."

Orli appeared soon after that, with about seventy old women trailing behind her. They had arrived with a transport from Slovakia and had been taken out of a Jewish old-age home. In my entire life I had never seen such old people. When we started registering them it turned out that the youngest of them was sixty-eight years old. They all wore wide, black, ankle-length skirts. In the past they would have gone straight from the wagons to the crematorium. But today Mengele told us to receive them on the hospital block. We looked at each other in disbelief. Something strange was going on around us, but we did not know what.

Some women were so old they could not sit. They lay on stretchers, waiting for the arrival of Mengele. Orli was as surprised as we were. She also did not know the reason for the change.

"See how the wolf has changed into a lamb," she said.

I must admit to some ugly thoughts that I remember buzzing through my head: "Such beautiful, young, healthy women had been sent to the gas chambers, and these women who are barely living, wrinkled, wilted, and old, will avoid death." How could I think that way, as if I had something against those old people to whom life had been granted as a present?

We finished registering the newcomers. When Mengele came in, Orli shouted, "Achtung!" But he just made a wave with his hand. He was looking at the registration card of one of the old women who was sitting in a corner when she yelled out, "God bless you for your goodness, that you take such pains to protect us old people."

Mengele shuddered and quickly looked in our direction. We lowered our heads so that he could not read anything in our eyes.

"Why are you blessing me before you know me?" he asked in a rage.

The old lady took fright from the tone of his voice; luckily she knew enough to keep quiet.

A number of stretchers were near the door of the infirmary, and in them were lying a few old people who had fallen very ill after the trip.

"Give them an injection of phenol," Mengele said to Orli. "Why should they suffer?" Smiling, he looked at Orli and waited for an answer.

"I don't know how to give such injections. That is your specialty," she answered instantly.

"Orli, I'm going to give you some good advice. Forget what you've seen here."

"Niemals [never]," Orli answered, without thinking.

One day late in November of 1944 we received a visit from Hans, an Austrian comrade. This summer the resistance had arranged to get him assigned to the *komando* working on the train ramp. They wanted him to inform the new prisoners arriving in Auschwitz what was awaiting them in the showers. He barely escaped the gas chamber himself, because the skeptical prisoners began to question the SS men in order to corroborate the information he had given them. Having succeeded in eluding the SS, he had come, now, to visit us, cheerful and full of positive thoughts, as ever. He brought me as a present a beautiful winter coat, which I sold in April of 1945 in Rostock for a loaf of soggy bread and half a box of margarine.

As so often happened, we got into a discussion on the future of the camp. Hans had brought us interesting news. The Red Army had crossed the Prussian frontier and the fighting was taking place on German soil.

"That's why they stopped the gassing in Auschwitz," Hans said. "They are afraid that the Germans may suffer the same fate. It seems that the Russians have given them an ultimatum about that."

Now I understood why Mengele had not sent those decrepit old people to the gas. The rulers of the world were afraid, those same rulers who, as early as July 1941, had painted signs in big white letters on their trucks: "Berlin-Moscow." Although the war was not yet over, they were being forced to yield and to make an attempt to placate the winners.

It was in the waning hours of a short fall day that Orli came into the infirmary. "Have somebody stand at the gate and guard the entrance," she said. "I will give you a copy of the latest issue of Goebbels's newspaper, *Das Reich*, in which a speech by Ilya Ehrenburg is reprinted."

At first I thought that I must have heard it wrong. How could that be? Goebbels printing an article by Ehrenburg? Maybe he had printed it as a provocation.

"Read it," Orli insisted. "You will see."

"*Wehe, Deutschland!*" "Woe unto Germany!" That was the title of the article. The article was prefaced with a few words by the editor and ran as follows: "An article appeared in the Russian newspaper, addressed to the Russian soldiers who had entered German territory. We are reprinting it in its entirety in order to show you what is awaiting us in case we lose the war. We are printing it to warn our soldiers and to arouse their manhood in the fight against the Bolsheviks. For us there is no turning back!"

Following this preface came Ilya Ehrenburg's article. I quote the article from memory, but I have read it so many times that I can recall the sense of it fairly accurately:

Soldiers of the Red Army [wrote Ehrenburg], you have entered the territory of Hitler's Germany. You are on the road to Berlin. Take revenge for everything, for what you the people of the Soviet Union have suffered and for what the other occupied peoples have had to suffer. Take revenge for all the suffering inflicted by the Germans.

In case pity for the Germans should creep into your hearts, remind yourselves of your mothers dragged by the hair, your sisters who were raped by the brutes, children whose heads were split open on lamp posts. Be merciless avengers! Quaff the sweet wine of revenge and let it fill your hearts.

Our own hearts now filled with the yearning for revenge, revenge for our wasted young lives, for the death of our relatives, for the red sky, for the acrid stench of burning flesh that was with us day and night.

When we switched on the electric light we saw that Orli was no longer among us. She had slipped quietly into the infirmary, and now she was sitting in the corner, with her head on the table, crying in despair.

"Understand," she said as we approached her, "those are my people. It is my nation that is fallen into misfortune. My brothers are there, my parents and my sisters."

We did not say a word.

"My soul is being torn apart," she said finally.

THE NEW YEAR'S CELEBRATION

There was a line in front of the mirror hanging on the wall. Everyone wanted to look good tonight. We were all excited, as if we were going to a grand ball. We had to make a celebration of greeting the new year, 1945.

In December we had already decided to celebrate the new year merrily. We were sure that the year 1945 would bring with it the defeat of Germany and that the Russian offensive would sweep away the camp in Auschwitz. Of this much we were certain, but it was difficult to foresee what would happen to us. On this day, however, we did not want to think about that. We had decided that today we would have a good time, just like people throughout the world.

We decorated the infirmary to give it a festive look. We set tables covered with white tablecloths in the middle of the room. On the table were all sorts of dainties that Lucy had been preparing for days. She was the superintendent of the kitchen in the area. The girls had brought her whatever they could manage to grab. Some of us had even hoarded our bread just to make sure that there would not be a shortage at the New Year's Eve party. Everyone had an assigned place at the table. On each plate lay a card with the name and next to it a beautifully painted branch of a pine tree. By each plate lay a star intended as a souvenir. In addition to this there were presents that we gave to each other. I remember that I received a keepsake from Orli, and I had also "organized" something for her. It had cost me a great deal of effort, but I finally managed to get her a beautiful, colored silk scarf.

Next to my table lay a beautifully wrapped package: "For dear Sara, from Orli." Finally, we were all assembled, except for one of the girls who had to stand guard duty in front of the infirmary. Lucy performed the function of hostess. With a pleasant smile she conducted each person to her place. She set a bottle of wine in the middle of the table. "Where did she get it?" I thought with amazement. We called Lucy the ambassador from Luxembourg because she was the only representative of that small kingdom. She was tall, slim, and pleasant. That day she put on a performance that surprised us. We had no idea she was so clever.

We were all sitting at the table when Eva, the first person on guard duty, burst in: "Girls, come and take a look. Something strange is happening in the camp." We all ran out. The camp looked like a ghost town. There was nothing but snow, frost, and silence.

"Do you remember what it used to be like in the camp on New Year's Eve? The place used to be full of the singing and roaring of drunken Germans. All night there was nothing but shooting and shouting. The camp orchestra used to play for them all night so they could dance until dawn. Where are they now? Are they hiding someplace? Have they just run away?"

The solitude and the deathly calm were making us uneasy. There was no point in guarding the entrance of the infirmary. There was nobody around. We sat down to supper. We all admired the stars next to our plates. I received a beautiful two-colored sweater from Orli. The top was gray and the bottom brown. After dinner there was dancing, singing, and recitations in different languages. It was a loud, merry party. In a word, it was wonderful. I had not celebrated New Year's Eve since 1941. In the ghetto every new year brought us closer to extermination. There was no room for optimism. I remember that we did not even exchange good wishes. The angel of death was stalking and we felt that there was no way we could escape from him. Now I looked at the happy girls with feelings of unrestrained joy. I listened to the joyful songs and the happy voices. I went around kissing everyone. I believed that we would live through our ordeal and that eventually we would be happy.

Suddenly the door of the infirmary swung open and an SS man came barging in. We turned to stone. He had a pistol in his belt, and I waited for him to pull it out and start shooting at us. The intense silence coming on the heels of all the tumult of the party set our ears ringing. We stood in front of the table in order to conceal the food and the bottle of wine that was dominating the middle. The SS man took a few steps in our direction, and then we saw that he was drunk. He could hardly stand.

"Why are you all so quiet? Why don't you celebrate?" he blubbered. "I came here to celebrate with you. Hitler *kaput*," he roared at the top of his voice. "Long live Stalin." We looked at each other not knowing what to do. We feared a trap. "Don't be afraid of me. Celebrate! Nobody will come. Nobody is here." He sat at the table, and we also sat down. We decided not to interrupt the party. Lucy poured a glass of wine for everyone and then made a toast to our freedom: "Hitler *kaput*. Long live Stalin."

The Hungarian woman who conducted the camp orchestra was with us. She took up her violin and started playing sad songs mingled with bouncing gypsy melodies. Later she accompanied the Russian, French, and Polish songs that were sung by all those present. Finally we started to dance obereks, polkas, waltzes, tangoes, and anything else we could think of. Our uninvited guest also danced, punctuating his dancing every few minutes with shouts of "Hitler *kaput*."

The main event of the evening was to be a rendezvous with our men friends. At twelve o'clock we were to go to the barbed wire fence separating the women's camp from the men's. We had arranged this meeting a few days ago, with the understanding that we would come if it were at all possible to do so. Now our problem was what to do with the drunken SS man. What if he should suddenly sober up and start shooting? At the moment he was completely soused. He kept pulling a bottle out of the side pocket of his uniform, taking a healthy swig out of it each time. He smiled slightly and repeated, "Hitler lost the war. The end is near." We decided to risk it. Before twelve, Orli took him by the arm, offering to take him back to the guard house. But he did not want to go. "I will go with you," he insisted stubbornly. What could we do? We took him with us.

It was a cold night. Clean, soft snow was floating gently to the ground. The night was bright and silent. There was not an SS man in sight, except for the one who was dragging along behind us. Orli was supporting him on one side and Marusia on the other. We wanted to make sure that he would not shoot in the air, not even as a salute.

The snow was piled deep near the barbed wire. We sank in up to the waist. Our friends were already waiting at the fence.

"What kind of a bird is this? Where did you get the SS man?" they wondered at first.

We explained what had happened. Suddenly we heard a distant clock strike twelve. Somebody started singing the "Internationale." We all took up the melody in different languages. Each of us sang the song of triumph, the song of revolution in his or her native language.

Later we exchanged greetings and wished each other good cheer. We shook hands through the electrified fence. The SS man pushed himself toward the fence. We could hardly hold him back.

"Let him go," our friends joked. "Let him drop dead."

It was easy to joke like that, but we made sure he did not touch the fence. Later there were artistic performances, poetry, and songs. I sang Russian songs. There was applause, laughter, and congratulations.

At one point I thought that I was dreaming. Is it possible that all of this is really happening? Those fences; the "Internationale" ringing through the whole camp; those muffled yells of the SS man, "Hitler *kaput*"; our joy; and the taste of freedom that we felt in our hearts. That is how our dream of freedom and the defeat of Germany became a reality. The year 1945 was beautiful, filled with joy from the very first moment it began.

We were awakened by the sounds of rifle butts banging on the gates of the infirmary and by the yelling of the Germans.

"Open! Quick!"

We jumped out of bed. We put on whatever was at hand. We were so nervous that everything flew out of our hands.

"Open up quickly!" they screamed from the other side of the gate.

Dr. Koenig and a few SS men burst into the infirmary. They were dressed as if for a trip, with hats and rucksacks, and they were armed.

"Give us all the documents! Sick charts, the admissions books, everything! Don't hide anything," Koenig said threateningly.

We dragged out everything. An SS man was loading the papers into a big sack, which he would tie with a thick rope. Koenig was looking through all the cards. Then he looked at us as though he was considering something. He noticed our nervousness. It was simply too difficult for us to cover it up.

"Don't be afraid of anything," he said. "We won't leave you to the Bolsheviks."

Finally they left. They took the sack with them.

"He really comforted us," Kwieta joked.

We came out to the front of the infirmary. The snow and frost crunched underfoot. Echoes of artillery fire reached our ears from a distance. Every few minutes rockets illuminated the sky. The Germans were running from the camp. You could hear the murmur of the cars departing.

It was 17 January 1945. Hope tore at our hearts. Maybe the Germans really are fleeing, and maybe they are going to abandon us prisoners. That would have been the best solution.

"Don't delude yourselves," Orli tried to convince us. "The Germans won't leave us to the Bolsheviks. Either they will blow up the camp at the last minute or they will force us into other concentration camps. I know them very well. They will not let even one witness to their crimes survive! We have to be ready to march."

We constantly thought about whether we should let ourselves be evacuated. Maybe we should hide somewhere in the camp area and not run away with the Germans. The majority thought that the camp would be razed when the SS men left. All of the prisoners who thought so, and who could still drag their feet, "signed out" of the area and made ready for the trip. Liberation seemed so close, and yet we were still in mortal danger.

On the evening of 18 January the SS men gave us the signal to march. It was already dark when the prison guards started chasing us with dogs through the large gates with the sign, "Arbeit macht frei." The SS men attempted to count us, but they got mixed up. There was no time for a roll call. The explosions that seemed to be getting closer all the time were unnerving them. They were hurrying frantically and were terribly scared. We stood around completely unorganized before starting into the unknown. As we formed into a ragged column, SS men escorted us with dogs on each side of the column.

A cold wind was blowing and the frost crackled. The women dragged along slowly; many of them were sick and exhausted. Every minute shots resounded. The SS men shot the women who could not keep up with the march. The bodies were thrown onto the side of the road. We walked through a valley of death formed by the bodies of the prisoners. Apparently the men had walked here before us, because the valley of death was thickly planted with their corpses.

Every hour the SS men announced a ten minute rest. Wherever we were standing at the moment of the announcement, we would fall to the snow and fall asleep instantly. Later, when the march resumed, it was difficult to get up and drag one's self further. Slowly the night went by, and still we could not see the end of our trip.

Before dawn the SS men chased us into a village that was completely deserted.

"Here you will rest for a few hours," they said.

We fell into a barn and lay down in the straw. How wonderful. Maybe we could succeed in getting a little rest before continuing our march. We did not know how long the march would last. But we had not even managed to stretch out before we were dragged out to resume the march.

"Raus, raus," bellowed the Germans.

Maybe it was possible to dig into the straw and not move from the place. Maybe they would not notice, and I could stay in the straw until the war ended.

"Get up," Marusia nudged me.

"What for?" I answered in a whisper. "I will remain here."

"Do you really want to try?" she asked.

I didn't answer. Everybody left. I remained alone.

I heard the barking of a guard dog close by. I jumped up in haste and ran out of the barn. I did not want to be torn apart by a dog. In Auschwitz I had seen what a death like this was. Quickly I joined a file. Now I was alone, amongst women I did not know, and I would have nothing to depend on but my own strength. I was actually glad about it. The girls would not abandon me, but they were in danger, just like me. I had no strength for further wanderings. The skin was completely peeled from my feet. I could feel the blood swishing around inside my boots.

As we were leaving the village I saw two corpses in striped uniforms lying in the sand. They had no heads. I wondered feverishly what they had done to meet such a death. Maybe they tried to run away. Maybe they had killed an SS man. I dragged myself along by sheer force of will. Women were passing me by. I found myself almost at the end of the column. Behind me walked only the SS men. I was waiting for a bullet in the back of my head.

"Faster," one of them yelled to me.

"I can't, my feet are sore," I answered defiantly. I wanted to suppress the fear that was clutching my throat.

The SS man hurried his steps and stood in front of me.

"You don't want to live?" he asked. "You want me to kill you?"

"I don't want to die, but I guess I have to," I answered.

"Schade [A pity]," he said.

I was so surprised that I stopped in my tracks.

"What?" I thought. "Is he pitying me, a Jew who can barely drag her feet?" We looked at each other for a second in silence.

"What do we do with you?" he repeated as though to himself.

Suddenly, as if by magic, a sled drawn by two horses appeared along the side of the road. A peasant was driving, and next to him was a fat, rosy-cheeked woman dressed in warm fur and wrapped in a woolen shawl. On the sled were a few cans of milk.

"Halt," the SS man shouted.

The sled stopped.

"Where are you going?" he asked.

The peasant named the city. The couple on the sled were Germans.

"Take this prisoner on the sled. Take her to the city and leave her at the headquarters of the gendarmes," he ordered. "Go ahead," he said to me, "and don't try to run away." I got in. The sled started moving.

I was so bewildered by what had happened that I pinched my cheek to make sure that I was not dreaming. That bewitched sled, the surroundings in which it appeared, the SS man who stopped the couple so that I could ride with them, everything was so unreal that it could not happen in reality, only in a dream. Meanwhile, the sled was passing long columns of miserable women.

"Sara! Sara!" Marusia and Kwieta and others were calling to me, waving their hands happily, surely thinking that I must be getting away. How could I get away wearing a striped coat with a patch on the back? The sled passed the marching women and was soon at the head of the column. Leading the column were the commandant and his staff.

"Stop!" shouted the SS men, pointing their guns at the sled.

The sled stopped.

"My life in paradise is over," I thought. I said nothing. I did not explain. I would rather have the peasants speak. The woman told them that I had not gotten into the sled on my own, that the *obersturmführer* had told them to take me to the gendarmes. They fell into a quiet consultation among themselves about what to do with me. If the *obersturmführer* had ordered me into the sled he must have had a good reason. Nevertheless, it was not fitting that I should go by myself, so they put an SS man on the sled who was to be my escort.

The SS man was young; he tried to entertain me. He also wanted to find out who I really was.

"Have you known the *obersturmführer* for a long time?" he asked. "Do you like him?"

I kept my mouth shut, pretending to be dozing. We were going fast, and I felt cold.

"What can you cover yourself with?" my escort worried. "You are probably hungry, and I don't have anything on me to eat."

After a few hours of fast riding, we stopped at the German gendarmerie building. The peasants were happy to get rid of us, and they went quickly on their way. My escort and I entered the building housing the gendarmes. A chair was offered to me with great courtesy, and I sat down at the table.

The gendarmes were getting ready to evacuate. All of the papers had already been burned. They kept constantly bringing down large and small boxes. Everything was ready to be evacuated. I put my head on the table and fell asleep. Again I saw corpses without heads, alleys littered with dead bodies, and above it all, a red sky. Somebody poked me in the side. I jumped up, frightened. My escort was holding out a mess kit filled with aromatic soup.

"Here," he said, "eat." He brought me a spoon. How I savored that soup. It really had the taste of heaven. I ate every drop.

It was starting to get dark, but the women from the transport had not gotten there yet. Now I started worrying about the *obersturmführer*. It was bound to get out that I was not an esteemed prisoner and that the *obersturmführer* had ordered me onto the sled out of caprice. How could I avoid meeting him? I racked my brain.

It was completely dark when I saw the row of marching women in the distance. When the column reached the gendarmerie, I said to the SS man who was escorting me, with as much confidence as I could muster, "I will join the transport now." Without waiting for an answer I left the building. Once again I was with everyone.

THE CAMP BLANKET

We dragged ourselves along the highways for a few more days, until we reached a side station where flatcars were waiting for us, the kind that you ship lumber in. It is difficult for me to say how long the terrible walk lasted. I could no longer tell the difference between day and night. There was no food, and we quenched our thirst with snow, which was plentiful. At one point, someone in the escort brought the news that the Bolsheviks were getting closer. From that time on, the tempo of our wandering speeded up. Everybody mustered the last remaining ounce of strength; none of us wanted to fall behind just when freedom seemed so close.

As usually happens in situations of this kind, news traveled from mouth to mouth, which caused wings to grow on our shoulders.

"Listen," Zenia whispered into my ear while walking, "the Russian command sent out a special company of soldiers just to liberate the transport from Auschwitz. They will be here soon."

I believed what she was saying. I did not even ask where she heard the news. I listened for the echo of shots, and I waited for freedom.

Next to me two girls were talking about something very quietly. By their sad faces you could tell that the news was not very good.

"What happened?" I asked.

"Not far from here, on the side of the road," one of them explained, "is a little forest. The machine guns are already set up there. They will take care of us quickly."

"Don't babble nonsense," I said sharply. "There are too many of us. They wouldn't have time to cover their tracks. The escorts are afraid of the Russian army. They won't do it."

But anxiety remained. It was already dark when we found ourselves standing in front of the open railway cars. They started loading us onto the flatcars, which were slippery with ice. There was a chaos of squeezing, shrieking, beating, and shooting. I became separated from my friends. Someone pushed me from behind, and I found myself in the car. The first women to be herded into the car tried to sit down, but they had to get up quickly in order not to be trampled by the women who were being pushed in after them. We were squeezed into the car so tightly that we could not even move an arm or a leg. I thought to myself that if we had to travel this way for any distance nobody would survive. Standing motionless we would all freeze. I even imagined that we would all become one stony mass with many heads.

Before the train left, two older soldiers got into the cars. They were our escort. They set a little bench in the back of the wagon, sat down, and did not even look at us. They spoke quietly to each other in Hungarian. The train pulled out and picked up speed quickly. The wind almost tore our heads off. Our legs were burning, as if exposed to real fire. No one spoke, because it would have been impossible to hear. The pervasive death-like silence was broken only by the roar of the wheels and the whistle of the wind.

Not far from me stood two young Polish girls.

"Zosiu," one said to the other, "I am going to jump off the train. What about you?"

"I will jump after you," answered the other.

Slowly they moved to the wall of the wagon. My heart stopped beating out of fear. I wished they would succeed. In fact, it was possible to try to escape. The car was open, and the escort consisted of two Hungarians who had their own problems. I did not turn my head in their direction. I just listened very carefully.

"Where are you crawling, you louse?" I heard the German *kapo* call out. There followed a terrible beating with a stick. The girl fell on the floor. That was the end of her. She was trampled to death by the German functionaries.

"Hey, there!" one of them yelled to the escorts. "A woman died here. Can we get rid of the body? There is no room for it in the wagon."

"Throw her out," one of them answered.

"Hey, hop, hey, hop." The body of the young girl went flying out of the car. None of us said anything. No one could be found who reacted like a human being to this monstrous crime. Why did we keep quiet? After all, it was not fear that closed our mouths. They numbered about ten to fifteen, and we were more than a hundred. It was all part of the routine. In camp they were the ones who did the hitting, while we were the ones who got the beatings and who did not even have the right to defend ourselves or shield ourselves from the blows. That is what the camp had done to us. It had stripped us of the capacity to make a human gesture or to react normally when confronted by an enemy.

Once again the thumping of the wheels made the time go by. We passed by large estates and small towns. Everything was so dark that it was difficult for us to orient ourselves and figure out where we were. A noise reached my ears, some sort of whining explanation. A woman had seated herself because she could no longer stand. The criminals pounced on her.

"Hey, there. Escort!" shouted one of the *kapos*. "A woman died. Can we throw her out?"

Once again there was the thump of a body cast out of the car. Now this sound started to repeat itself often. I came to the realization that the *kapos* were killing the women and getting rid of the bodies so that they would have more comfortable accommodations. Maybe, I thought, they will kill us all. They would be by themselves, and then they would be able to lie down comfortably on the floor. I was standing far enough from the German *kapos*, separated from them by a crowd of women. My legs hurt terribly, and I dreamt of only one thing, to sit down. I wanted to sit just for a moment, a short moment. But to sit in this car was impossible.

My attention was drawn to a booth located between the cars; inside the booth was a bench. I was seized with a desire to get to the booth. I thought that I would sit down and leave behind this car where the criminals were killing women before our very eyes, instead of standing here silent and scared. This nagging idea even killed my fear; the soldier escorting us might think that I was trying to run away and he might gun me down. Slowly I moved to the back of the car, and without thinking I put one leg over and then the other. I was in the booth. I sat down. I was sweating like a church mouse. I had succeeded! I sat down on the bench. I stretched my legs out in front of me. No one told me to return; I could travel here quietly. I felt so good, so comfortable. I dozed off. The cold awakened me. Now I felt cold. I had nothing to cover myself with. The wind and frost were tearing my head off. I was freezing. In the car the bodies were packed tightly together and were warming each other. Here I was alone and there was no place to move. I was afraid that the Hungarian soldiers or the German *kapos* might notice me.

I blew into my hands. I rubbed my feet together, but that did not help much. Sleep, which I could not shake off, overcame me. I fell asleep. Then a knocking on the wall of the booth woke me up, and I heard a feeble whisper:

"Please, ma'am, don't sleep! It's dangerous. You will freeze."

At first I was sure that I must be dreaming, that I must be talking to myself. With all my might I tried to open my eyes and lift my wobbly head. But I could not. It was beyond my strength. I fell asleep again.

"Please, ma'am," a loud whisper and a knocking on the wall reached me as if through a fog. "Please stretch out your hand and take the blanket. Quick," the urging voice insisted from the other world. "Please don't think about it. Just stretch out your hand."

I stretched out my arm and someone from the car really handed me a gray blanket from the camp. It was not a dream after all. "There is somebody in the car," I thought, "who wants to help me. Somebody wants me to live." I threw the blanket over my head. I wrapped my back and chest and hid my hands.

Now I knocked on the wall of the booth. "Please, ma'am, you saved my life. I feel warm now. Do you need the blanket?"

"No," a whisper came back. "We had two blankets, my daughter and I. We covered ourselves with one, and we are warm."

How is this possible? I pondered. On one side such bestiality, and on the other unselfish love toward another creature. Then I realized that I did not even know my savior's name and that I would never be able to repay her for the gray blanket that, for me, meant the difference between life and death.

"Ma'am." I knocked again. "Please give me your name. I really must know your name." Silence. "Can you hear me?" I called out loud. "Please. Your name." "Your name, your name, your name," was repeated in the echo of the wheels.

"Stretch out your hand." I heard a whisper from behind the wall. I stretched out my hand. In my hand I found a dry crust of bread from the camp. I chewed it up and then let the dry crumbs dissolve in my mouth. "Your name, your name," I insisted.

"Your name, your name, name." The wind was blowing in my ears.

IN PURSUIT OF LIFE

n the afternoon we descended on Ravensbrück* like a swarm of locusts. Even here the word "Auschwitz" caused anxiety and fear. The prisoners here looked at us with fear in their eyes, because we were terrifying to see. The days of marching without rest, the terrible trip standing in the open railway car, hunger and thirst, the stink that hovered over our column—all this made us seem like shadows swaying down the road to Hell.

I searched the column for acquaintances, and I staggered along the side of the column like a wounded bird. It was impossible to recognize anybody. It struck me, then, that we had come to Ravensbrück only to die. They pushed us into a barrack. Nine women were assigned to one three-decker bed. The camp was in a state of total disarray. The evacuation of Auschwitz had unnerved the SS men. It took their minds off us. First of all, sleep. The need for sleep is stronger than hunger. We threw ourselves onto the beds, the floor, any place, like dead souls. I remember that the *blokowa* tried to count us. She kept yelling repeatedly, "Achtung!" The *sztubowe* were beating the sleeping faces, and we kept on sleeping. Finally they let us alone. After all, it was January 1945.

From the very first moment that we arrived in Ravensbrück, they were already talking about a transport that would take us further. There was no place to put us here. Everyone wanted to stay a little longer, to rest and to eat, even though the food was even worse here than in Auschwitz. We received a crumb of pasty bread in the morning, and then we waited for the soup that we received for lunch and supper. The soup had no fat in it, and you could sip endlessly without feeling even a dent in your hunger.

"What do you think?" asked Irka. "How many plates of this soup

---

*A concentration camp in eastern Germany, about fifty miles north of Berlin and twenty miles north of Sachsenhausen. It became a way station and dumping ground for dying captives on death marches as the Nazis tried desperately to finish their attempted genocide.

can you eat?" I thought very hard about this question. Then I told her, "I think I could eat it without end."

"You know what?" Irka continued, "This evening I will steal a can of soup from the kitchen. Those twenty-five liters. We'll eat, yes?"

There were four of us. We would have to consume the soup so nobody would notice and then put the empty can back in the kitchen.

"How will you do it?" asked Marusia.

"Simply. In the evening we will both go to the kitchen, pretending to get soup for a certain block. Right under the cook's nose I will throw her a block number that doesn't exist. She will pour the soup and we will hand it to you through the window." Our bed was located near the window.

"And if it doesn't come off?" Kwieta worried.

"The worst we will get is a rap on the head with the ladle. It's worth trying."

In the evening Irka and Marusia went to the kitchen, while Kwieta and I waited at the window. As we waited for them to show up our eyes almost popped out. Then we saw them walking in the middle of the road, carrying what looked like a thermos of soup. They made a spurt in our direction, and before we knew it the thermos was lying on our bed covered with a blanket. So as not to attract attention, we had to wait until supper time before we could eat our bottomless plate of soup. Finally, it was supper time. We sat on the bed eating barley soup. We hid the thermos near the window and kept refilling our plates with our cups, so that our plates were always full.

"So," Irka asked, "will you eat like this for a long time? My stomach is like a drum, but I still like the soup."

"I think," said the sweating Kwieta, "that we will not be able to finish the soup. Maybe we should offer some to the neighbors."

"No," we all answered. "They will think that we stole the can from the block and they will hit us, or they will complain to the *blokowa*."

We spent the whole night eating the soup in secret. Just before dawn we threw the empty thermos far from the barrack, in the middle of the road.

"We really had a feast," we told each other.

Every day transports left Ravensbrück. We knew that our turn would come.

"It would be good if you didn't have to go anywhere," Marusia once said to me. How did one organize this? I would have to come up with something. Actually, I did not feel well. I had wounds on my legs, which had gotten frostbitten during the evacuation. The transports were difficult. Only a healthy person could survive them. I was afraid of the transport, but there was no place to hide.

On the evening of that same day, Marusia returned from her wanderings in the camp very happy. First of all, she had found work for me in a repair shop where they mended the camp clothes. I could stay in Ravensbrück. The second bit of news elicited a shout of "hurrah" from us. In Ravensbrück there were no French girls, no Sonias or Evas. They had stayed in Auschwitz. Orli, whom Marusia had met, told her that Auschwitz had already been liberated. The Germans did not blow it to bits. They did not have time. The Russian army was there. "Hurrah," yelled Kwieta. "Hurrah." We had tears in our eyes.

Why had we let ourselves be evacuated? Why had we not stayed in Auschwitz? We had feared for our lives, and during the evacuation our lives were hanging by a hair. What lay in wait for us? How many evacuations and transports full of fear and suffering did we still have to bear? Letting ourselves be evacuated was a false step on our part, I thought, for which we would have to pay.

The next morning I went to the workshop. It consisted of a large room with a long table in the middle. On the table were piles of torn clothes. The women sat at the table with needles in their hands. The work was easy. Marusia had really pulled it off. The *kapo* from the shop greeted me cordially. At last I had it made. I thought, I will be able to survive here until the war ends. In the evening the girls told me that they had reported themselves for the transport. In that way, they thought, they would all go together. The next day, after roll call, they all left. I was left alone.

I cried under the blanket at night. I was not used to being alone. In the camp the wall separating one human being from another was sometimes so thin that it was transparent. That was how close I felt to the girls who left that day. Would I be able to manage in this strange camp among these unfamiliar women? In the morning, after roll call, I went to the shop and I did not return to the block until evening. The days went by in Ravensbrück. I had been there for three weeks. Then, unexpectedly, the shop was closed. One day, just as we were sitting down to mend the clothes, an SS man came storming in with whip in hand.

"The mending is all over. Get out of here," he screamed.

As we stood, stunned and indecisive, at the table, he started hitting us on the head with the whip. We barely managed to get out of there with our lives. I took a few steps and stood in the middle of the road, not knowing what to do. Where should I go now? Where could I hide? I knew that as soon as I got back to the block they would chase me to the transport. "What do I do, now," I thought, with despair in my heart.

I reminded myself that Dr. Frumka worked in the Ravensbrück area. She had been with us for a long time in Auschwitz, and then, before the evacuation, she had left to go to Ravensbrück.

Frumka was an unusually fine person. Her entire being glowed with nobility and honesty. I had to find her. She would certainly help me. I went from block to block, inquiring about her of anyone I met. Finally, after a few hours, I was shown the block where Dr. Frumka worked.

At the entrance the orderly stopped me.

"Frumka is sick. She has pneumonia. She is in bed in the area. Go to the window. I will send her to you," she finished, seeing my troubled face.

I stood at the window, feeling that the last straw I could cling to had sunken into the deep. Frumka appeared, looking quite wretched. Quickly I told her everything.

"I have been sick and confined to bed for two weeks now," she told me. "I haven't been working, so I can't check you into the hospital. What shall I do with you?" she concluded worriedly.

I looked around carefully, looking for a hole I could hide in. I was afraid to go back to the block, but I was not allowed to stay there any longer. Frumka started thinking aloud, casting about for a solution, and her words drifted to my ears as through a fog. Suddenly a thought struggled to the surface which made me feel

as light as if a ton of bricks had fallen from my shoulders. Why
was I worrying so much about my rotten life? If I had a child with
me, or another person who was close to me, then I might have
had some reason to worry. But since I was alone, let fate take its
course. What will be will be. Even today I remember how all my
worries left me and I felt as free and as light as a bird.

"Goodbye, Frumka," I said with a laugh, and I left.

"Wait, you maniac," Frumka shouted. "Where are you going?
Tell me what you have decided."

I did not answer her. I just waved my hand to her. The struggle
for life bored me. I returned to the block, and an hour later I was
aboard a transport. I was given half a loaf of bread, a piece of
salami, and I did not give a damn about what might happen after
that.

A large military airport with underground hangars. Next to it stood about fifteen barracks buildings that once housed French workers who had been brought to Germany to do forced labor. They had worked as maintenance personnel. Later the workers had been sent elsewhere, because the German military was afraid of sabotage. The barracks had been standing empty for a year. They brought our transport from Ravensbrück to this barracks in Rostock.

When we entered the gates of the new camp in the middle of February, we were greeted not only by the camp officers and the SS hierarchy but also by the grim faces of the Auschwitz functionaries: the *blokowe*, the clerks, and the *sztubowe*. When I first saw them I thought that my exhausted mind must be hallucinating, but that was not the case at all. They were the same well-dressed, fully rested, attractive Auschwitz functionaries. They looked at us not only with contempt but with anger.

"Would you believe it?" one of them said to me later. "They brought us here a week before you arrived. We cleaned the barracks. We made the place look like a model camp. And then they go and bring in old, miserable, stinking women. In a word, old sick women. It's just not right to bring them to an ideal German camp, which is what they were going to create here in Rostock. All the old functionaries—the *blokowe*, the *kapos*, the clerks—took the nice, cozy rooms for themselves."

The barracks were all built the same. A narrow corridor ran down the middle of the building for its entire length. Stalls were on both sides. At the end of the corridor was a toilet and a wash room. In the main room there were twenty-four three-decker beds, twelve on each side of the corridor. In the corridor stood a table and two benches. Two women slept in each of the narrow beds. The room had windows, but they were blocked by the beds so that they could not be opened, and they did not admit any light. Seventy-two women slept in this overcrowded room. Is it any wonder that the stench was terrible, and that after a few days we were crawling with lice?

In Rostock I came to understand why one of the plagues that God sent on the Egyptians was lice. This was a plague in whose presence we were helpless. The lice were big and white, each with a black cross on its back. They feasted on us day and night. This was an enemy whom you had to fight—search and destroy. When I went to the bathroom at night I would see women standing near the electric lamp that gave off a faint light, searching for lice in their clothes. One would leave her position near the light, and immediately someone would take her place.

"Don't be embarrassed," an elderly lady whispered in my ear, "otherwise the lice will eat you up."

"How will they eat me?" I asked, frightened.

"They'll eat you up," she said, "the way they ate this girl in the first bed."

The next day I looked at the young woman. She lay in bed motionless, semiconscious, covered with scabs. Even during the day she did not move from her bed. In Rostock there was no assembly area, and the old Auschwitz regimen no longer existed there either. The sick just lay in the block. This young woman just lay there with the lice crawling all over her. They were devouring her alive. She was unable to fight them. What could we do? She died.

Although you did not have to go to work here, some women kept busy cleaning the camp. It seemed as if this camp had been opened just to give the SS men an excuse for not going to the front. All day we sat in the barracks and thought about food. We knew that the war would end soon, but we did not think about freedom, we thought about food. The hunger in Rostock was absolute. In the morning we received a cup of black coffee, and every few days we were given a spoon of sugar. Lunch was at twelve. We took our plates to the kitchen. Outside, an SS man poured soup from a can and gave us a piece of soggy bread. The soup was always the same, cooked with dry roots, without salt, and that was all. Is it any wonder that hunger gnawed at our intestines and did not allow us to think about anything else but a piece of bread?

I slept in the same bed with Klara, an eighteen-year-old girl from Lodz. After lunch, when the soup and bread had been consumed, and the hunger had subsided for a few minutes, we spoke about freedom. We tried to foresee the form in which freedom would come to us. I decided not to let myself be evacuated. After all, where could they take us? The future was painting itself in pink colors if we could only bear the lack of food which was turning us into *mussulmen*. Every morning when I washed my emaciated body in the wash room I looked at myself in horror; chest straight as a board, legs like sticks. If the war did not end in the next few months I would not live through it. Of that I was certain.

One day the *blokowa* started talking to me. She proposed that I sell her my winter coat. I had a really nice coat, a sports coat with a very nice fur collar. I got it from friends in Auschwitz.

"What do you mean, sell it to you?" I asked, wondering.

"Simple," she answered. "I will give you a loaf of bread and a package of margarine for it."

Instantly I said, "No!" angrily. Look, I thought, we are starving and she is stealing bread, and she has so much of it that she can buy a coat with it.

After that, I could not get the vision of a loaf of bread and a package of margarine out of my mind. If the war lasted until winter I would not be alive anyway, so what did I need the coat for? It was warm now and I did not need it. One morning I took the coat and exchanged it for the bread and the margarine. Klara and I ate the bread and margarine for lunch. After the feast, Klara said, "We ate the coat."

That is what April 1945 was like. Very often we were awakened at night by the wailing of sirens and by the dull echo of bombs falling somewhere. You could sense the alarm coming from the nearby airport. We could hear the planes taking off, and we felt overwhelmed with joy. We, on these lice-ridden beds, belonged to the victors. We knew it for sure. In the middle of April the airport was bombed and the hangars were damaged. The day was nice, warm, and bright. We drank the warm dishwater that passed for coffee and waited for lunch.

Suddenly a silver plane appeared above the camp. It circled above us and then left. The sky over the camp was crisscrossed with white streaks, as if someone had painted a checkerboard on the sky with white paint. Later, the bombers arrived. The whole barrack started vibrating. The earth trembled. All Hell broke loose. We lay stretched out on the floor.

"Don't be afraid." I tried to calm the women. "Do you see the markings in the sky? That's so they won't drop bombs on the camp."

The bombing lasted all day. As the bombers departed they dropped millions of leaflets. There were so many of them that they covered the sun as they fell, leaving us in shadow. The commandant and the SS men ran through the camp like madmen: "You are not allowed to read the leaflets. We will shoot you if you do." There were so many leaflets that their order had a comic ring to it. The leaflets proclaimed: "The war is ending. You will be free in a few days." There was also a detailed map showing where the Allied forces were located. They could not really ship us out. There was just no place to go. We did not get lunch that day, but who was thinking about food? We were dreaming about a map of Germany. There was Rostock, with the Russian, British, and American armies marching in our direction.

You know what?" Wierka came running from the next room after breakfast. "I will tell you something wonderful. You will see. You will faint from excitement."

At that time we were sipping the hot dishwater, which burned our empty stomachs, and we paid no attention to her words. Wierka was a young, happy Ukrainian girl, a known prankster; she liked to tease us, to frighten and confuse us with unusual news.

"You don't want to hear?" she asked further. "I swear to God that I am not teasing. From now on they will have to give us the food packages sent for us by the Red Cross."

I stopped sipping for a minute. "I suppose someone gave you some secret information about it," I said.

"Really, I found out about it from a good source. Believe me. After all, you will find out for yourself."

She ran out of our room in order to carry the news to the others.

Klara said, "She knows what she's talking about."

The end of April 1945 was approaching. It was warm and sunny. We saw that the war would soon be ending. We believed that we would wait for the end of the war in Rostock. We hoped that the hunger and the lice would not finish us off. Our attending SS men did not pay the least attention to us any more. Even the *blokowe* did not care about us. We wandered around the camp dreaming and fantasizing about that day we were all talking about when the Red Cross packages would arrive. I did not know whether Wierka spread the news widely or whether the other women found out about the packages from another source. The next minute we would not believe the news, and we would dismiss Wierka's stupid talk with a disdainful wave of the hand.

We were really surprised when, after lunch, the *blokowe* told us to line up by twos and to march to the warehouse for packages. We marched accompanied by the functionaries. Wierka ran from one prisoner to another, saying, "Didn't I tell you? And you laughed at me." What kind of packages? And where did they come from? It was long after the war had ended that I found out that these packages were sent to the camps by way of the neutral countries and that the SS men in the concentration camps did not distribute them to the prisoners. They said that they were putting the contents into the cauldrons. Maybe they really did pour the contents into the cauldrons but into the cauldrons in which they cooked their own food. Now they had a large stockpile, and apparently they did not want the Allies to find unopened food packages in the camp while the inmates were dying of starvation. Each pair of prisoners approaching the table received a package, which they were supposed to divide between themselves. Klara and I received one package. We had no trouble dividing it because we ate together anyway. There were many quarrels, and even fights, when it came to dividing the packages.

In the packages there were crackers, sardines, ham, bacon, salami, sugar, cookies, and candy. The women threw themselves on the food. It was hard to control one's self and not eat. After so many months, and even years, without proper food, the stomach was no longer equipped to digest fats and sugar, so our digestive tracts rebelled immediately. It was devilish of the SS to give us all that food at once, knowing we would not be able to digest it. Many of the women became very ill.

The next day, 30 April, we did not receive the black dishwater when we went outside. The warehouses were open, and anyone who was able dragged out sugar, flour, and groats. There were no SS men. We thought that they had run away and left us alone. Not long after that, the camp commander appeared accompanied by SS men carrying carbines. The signal was given to evacuate the camp. We wondered where they were chasing us to now, and why they were evacuating us. We had to leave the barracks since there was no place to hide. But I decided that I would take the first opportunity to stay behind. I believed that there would be many such opportunities.

At first we took the side road that led out of the camp. Later, we reached the main road and stood there as though glued to the spot. The entire road was filled with fleeing Germans. Women and children, old people, on foot, on bicycles, in carriages drawn by horses. Mixed in with the people were cows, pigs, sheep, chickens in cages. Everyone was moving ahead as fast as he or she could. They had packages slung on their backs and valises hanging from hands and shoulders. Their faces were blackened with deathly fear and fatigue. I knew such roads, and I knew the blackened faces. September 1939 and April 1941 shimmered before my eyes, a living remembrance.

We stood on the side road while the female commandant and the SS men conferred on what to do with us. They were trying to figure out some way to work us into the crowd. Finally, it was decided we had to melt into the crowd in pairs, not knowing where we were going. Now I began to realize how difficult it was going to be to separate from the convoy. Along one side of the road, in a valley, stretched a green field fragrant with the aroma of spring. A short distance from the road stood large stacks of last year's hay. If it were possible for one to get to the stacks, one could hide there.

On the grass near the road, two men in camp suits were cooking potatoes in a big pot. They had built a fireplace with four bricks. Under the pot the fire was crackling merrily. The men were crouched around the pot. They were not worried.

"What are you doing?" I asked like a fool.

"What do you mean?" one of them answered. "We are cooking potatoes."

"Why are you standing there?" the other said. "Take a few steps down and crouch next to us. Nobody will notice you. We did that yesterday, and as you see, we didn't even bother to change our striped uniforms. The only thing they are interested in right now is in getting rid of you and saving their own skins."

I dragged Klara with me, and a moment later we were kneeling next to the pot of cooking potatoes. My heart was beating rapidly. I was terribly frightened. Slowly the column went by.

One of them said to us, "Now go to the hay stacks and hide in a hole. Just be careful not to trample anybody."

I did not understand what they had in mind, but we went to the stacks. You really had to be careful not to step on someone, because the whole stack was full of people, like an Easter dough full of raisins. Transports of prisoners had passed this way before us. These were workers who had been sent to forced labor and who had managed to separate themselves from their bosses. A hole was found for us also. I lay down on my back, my whole body pulsating with fear. The vision of the scene of horror I had witnessed on the road continued to pass before my mind's eye. I had to keep repeating aloud, "Look, the Germans are fleeing," in order to keep believing what I had seen. "Vengeance is a joy of the Gods." I had never experienced such happiness before. Finally, they have been touched by defeat, and they were running the way we had earlier. Then I remembered that we had been bombed by German planes and that they had strafed us with machine-gun fire; every few minutes we had had to run from the road into the fields. But no one was bothering these Germans in their panicked flight.

Klara interrupted my train of thought. "Look," she said, "there is a barracks in the back. The workers probably lived there. Maybe we'll find something to eat there."

We went to the barracks. There was no food, but the stove was still hot and on top of the stove stood a pot of hot water. We also found a large bowl, some soap, and a towel. We undressed and washed with hot water for the first time in many months. I could savor the taste of freedom. I stuck my face into the hot water and I wanted to scream with joy. I lifted my head and was struck speechless with fright. "Klara, look!" I screamed. I spotted an SS man walking in our direction.

He was so covered with soot that he was black from head to toe. You could not distinguish a face under that pile of dirt. Only his eyes shone with unusual luster. He had a pistol and grenades in his belt.

"The end," said Klara.

He went into the kitchen as if he had not seen us.

"So what?" he asked. "They let you out?"

He recognized that we were from the camps, even though we were without our striped uniforms.

"They let us out," I answered.

He gazed around with a crazed look.

"Give me bread," he said quietly.

"We were looking for bread ourselves, because we are also hungry. But there's no bread here."

"No bread?" he said.

He left.

"Oof," said Klara, "we've been spared."

We abandoned the barracks and hid in the hay stack.

THE FIRST DAYS OF FREEDOM

In those last few months I happened to find myself in peculiar situations. These situations were so far from anything logical that I could not believe in their reality. First there was the bizarre New Year's Eve celebration of 1945, when, surrounded by electric fences, we inmates of the concentration camp joined in camaraderie in singing the "Internationale." Then there was the enchanted sled that the *obersturmführer* put me into when I could not walk any farther; and the blanket that warmed my freezing body, which was given to me by an outstretched hand in the darkness. And now, 1 May 1945, there I was between Röbel and Rostock. Behind the stack, on the side away from the road, we placed a long, massive table and two benches that we had dragged out of the barracks on the evening of the first day. The table was used by the tenants of all those holes in the huge haystack. There was Sasha, a Russian, a tall blond man with a laughing face; Rene, a Frenchman, short and fat, and very witty; Irene and Janek, Poles, brother and sister, from Lodz. There was also an older Jewish woman with a twelve-year-old daughter, a sweet, pretty girl. She had come to Auschwitz in the summer of 1944, from the Lodz Ghetto, and miraculously succeeded, without any help, in smuggling her daughter into the camp and later in placing her on the block. Now they were together, and the mother's happiness knew no bounds. Further down the table sat two men from Poznan. They described themselves as professional pickpockets. All the day before they had been busy dragging valises full of goods from the nearby town. "We are taking back from the Germans what they took from us," they said. Finally, there was a Hungarian woman and a Slovak woman, and, not least, Klara and I.

On the table there was a large bowl of potatoes, standing next to a pot of horse meat and a pitcher of red borscht. In front of us were plates, spoons, and cups. Sasha was talking about May 1. He made a toast to the Red Army, which had frightened the Germans, so that now they were running away. We all lifted our cups of

borscht and raised them to our lips. I looked at the table, at these
people, my kindred creatures. I listened to the noise coming from
the highway, and again I got the feeling of fantasy, as though I
were dreaming a beautiful dream of freedom. "Now the 'Internationale,'" says Irene. Very few of those present actually knew the
song, but everybody stood, and those who did not know the song
listened as those of us who did sang in three languages: Russian,
Polish, and French.

As soon as we had finished singing we put everything back
in the barracks and resumed our hiding places in the haystack.
There was a constant stream of people on the road: civilians
mixed with soldiers, cows and horses alongside military cars and
armor. Dusk started falling slowly. We wondered when the Russians would get here and really set us free.

It was already dark when the two men from Poznan came back
with their packages. They were very upset, and started backing off
right away.

"Where are you going?" I asked anxiously.

"Down the road. There's a bridge not far from here. We're going
to cross it with the Germans. We found out that the bridge will be
blown up, and the battle is going to be fought right on this field.
It's dangerous to stay here. Run away, like we are doing."

"What?" everybody asked. "You expect us to run with the Germans?"

It was certainly dangerous to remain there. The bridge was only
about fifty meters from the haystacks. On the other side of the
river we could see cannons and guns. Apparently, the Germans
were going to try to prevent the Russians from crossing the river.
No one told anyone what to do. Each person made his or her own
decision individually. Late in the evening the two pickpockets
with their heavy valises went in the direction of the road. The rest
of us remained in the haystacks. No one slept or talked. We were
waiting for the roar that would destroy the bridge. We were most
reluctant to die now that we had tasted the intoxication of freedom. Trucks full of soldiers were constantly traveling along the
main road. There were now fewer civilians than there had been in
the morning. Finally, the ground started to rock beneath us, and

finally the bridge blew up. The stack was not damaged, and we were all intact. We were under a great deal of strain, and the blowing up of the bridge made us realize how exhausted we were. We fell asleep. A terrible roar woke me up. The whole field was illuminated. Grenades exploded in front of us and behind us. If one of them were to make a direct hit on the stack it would be the end of us all. There was no place to hide. We were as exposed as the bullseye of a target. The bombardment lasted all night without pause. Thus, on the threshold of freedom, I lived through the most dangerous night of my life.

At dawn the shooting stopped. Janek wanted to leave the stack to see what had happened. He slipped out of the stack and was gone for a long time.

"Come out," we heard him calling. "There are Russian soldiers all around us."

We climbed out of our holes. Truly, the grass was red with the stars on the soldiers' hats. They were holding their guns, ready to shoot. They surrounded us, full of suspicion. Only when they learned that we were prisoners of Auschwitz and other concentration camps did they let us go free.

"Wait here. We will come right back to take you across the pontoon bridge."

The village they took us to was full of soldiers. We looked around for an unoccupied hut in which we could wash up and get some sleep. Even hunger took a back seat. On the way we were stopped by a Russian captain. He asked about Auschwitz.

"How did you bear all this?" he kept asking every minute. "Do you have food?" We were amazed by the question. "Wait. I will find something for you."

A huge pig was waddling down the middle of the road. Our captain took out his gun. He fired and said: "Here is your food."

I was lying in a wide bed, covered with a German comforter. We had burned our camp uniforms in the garbage. An end to the lice. We had scoured ourselves and dressed in some old clothes that we had found in a house. The only thing I saved from the flames was the camp skirt, a gray garment with a big white cross painted on the back. I kept this as a remembrance. I felt comfortable, warm and clean. But I was not happy. I did not know why. Again and again I repeated to myself the refrain: "Be happy, you are free." But this did not help. I was sad. Sadness strangled me.

Lying there under this big German comforter I realized the tragedy of my situation; I was alone, no one was waiting for me, there was no one to return to. A plant can flourish only in its native soil, and I had been brutally torn out of mine. Of what value was the life that I had struggled so hard to redeem from Hitler's Hell? At this moment I did not know what to do with it.

I remember 9 May very clearly—the day the Germans surrendered. We still lived in the village, close to the front. We occupied a very nicely furnished house. Living in the same house were the older lady with her daughter, and the Hungarian and Slovak ladies. It was very early in the morning when the announcement was made. There was a banging on the door with rifles and carbines. We were very frightened but started to open the door. About twenty soldiers rushed into the room: "Girls, the war is ended! The Germans surrendered!" They took us in their arms and threw us up into the air. I was flying up and down, and the whole world was whirling around.

"I lived through Auschwitz! I will return to Lublin!" I repeated over and over again. Later we drank whisky for the living and the dead. We cried and laughed alternately. We wondered whether we could live normal lives like other human beings. Would my dreams be realized in recompense for my enormous suffering?

THE ROAD BACK

"Do you know what," the older lady from Lodz said to me, "I will tie your feet to these bars, because we could have an accident." Through my sleep I felt her tying my legs to the bars with a scarf. "The car is open, and if it should give a sudden jerk you could go flying." I heard her subdued voice through the roar of the wheels. "Mrs. is sleeping in a sitting position," she said, "and there could be a misfortune because it is easy to fall off. But the scarf will hold you."

Actually, I was not sleeping, only napping. I dozed on and off, dreaming a little. I was satisfied that I was headed for home. I did not have a home to return to this very minute, but I would certainly have one in Poland, in this new people's Poland. The trip on an open car was not comfortable, especially with the bars pinching my flesh, but I was moving forward, and for me that was the most important thing right then. It was no easy matter for me to get on this train in the first place.

Right after 9 May, Klara and the Hungarian woman came down with stomach typhus. A military ambulance took them to the hospital in Röbel. The next day I started getting ready to return to my country. I prepared myself psychologically only, because any other means was out of the question. Every day I went to the station with the older lady and her daughter, counting on some lucky break that would enable me to get back to my country. I felt myself suffocating in this little German town. I could not bear to look at the women in their white aprons, working in their gardens, carrying on their calm, normal, everyday lives.

I always took my possessions with me: one new sheet and a white tablecloth with a monogram in the corner. We did not have much food, but at that point I was not really interested in food. All I cared about was finding a way to get home.

I remember the twenty-first of May. As usual, we came to the station very early. I wandered out onto the tracks and saw a long line of cars loaded with iron bars. There was a convoy of Russian soldiers accompanying the shipment of iron bars. I thought to myself, where can such a train be going, and quickly I found the answer. It must be going to the Soviet Union. If it is going to the Soviet Union, what direction must it take? It must go through Poland. Without any further thought I took a seat on the bars. My friend and her daughter climbed in with me.

The train gave a sudden lurch, and we were underway. We passed fields, forests, and meadows with grazing cows. It looked quite idyllic, but that very fact troubled me. The tranquility is unbelievable. How could life return to its normal patterns so quickly?

After about an hour the train stopped at a station. A young Russian soldier told us that we had to get off. "This is a military transport," he said, "and civilians aren't allowed to travel on this train." What could we do now? We got off at the station, and when the soldier left we got on the train once more. At the next station we ran into the same problem. The soldier screamed, explained, ordered, but he could not guard all the cars at the same time, and as soon as he turned away from us we returned to the iron bars.

That was how we spent the first night on the iron bars. I did not even have a blanket to cover myself, and it was a cold night. In spite of the cold, I dozed, and the older lady tied my legs to the bars so I would not fall off the train. At night the train stopped for long stretches, moved a little, and then stopped again. If the train kept moving at this pace, I did not know whether I would be able to endure the trip. For food we had just one loaf of bread and a few pieces of sugar. If we had to stay on the train for a few weeks, what would we do then?

"Oh, ma'am," the older lady said to me, "here comes the soldier. He is going to chase us out of the car." We went down without being told, and a minute later we were back on the bars. This cat and mouse game with the soldiers made me angry. When the soldier appeared again at lunch time in order to repeat, "Citizens, you can't travel here," I asked him if he knew where we were returning from.

"I am a Communist," I shouted from the train. "I am rushing back to my country because they are building a Socialist state there. Think! Maybe they need me there, and you just keep chasing me and harassing me, instead of finding out whether I am hungry." I knew the Russian language very well, and anger gave wings to my words. Then, for the first time, I looked at his face. He was so young. He could not have been more than eighteen years old. He looked at me in astonishment, as if seeing me for the first time. I smiled at him and he answered me with a smile. He turned and left.

"Did you make things any better?" my friend asked. He would probably bring an officer who would chase us off the train for good. But he did not bring anybody. That evening he brought us half a loaf of army bread, some hot coffee, and a plate of soup. Later he brought a mattress and two blankets. We arranged ourselves in a booth between cars where it was warmer and safer. From that time on he brought us food every day. He did not ask questions. He just brought the food and left. Apparently, he was not supposed to speak to us.

At one of the stations, two Polish soldiers jumped into our car. They were dressed in Polish uniforms, with eagles on their hats. I rubbed my eyes, not believing what I was seeing. Polish soldiers. Where did they come from?

"Lady, why are you so surprised?" one of them asked. "You crossed the Polish border, ma'am. This is Poland," he repeated, seeing that I had turned to stone.

I remember that at that very moment I smelled a different aroma coming in from the fields. The sky looked different above us; different roads, forests, meadows, all rushed by the train. How is it possible that I had not noticed? I was overwhelmed with joy. I started to sing, to shout with joy.

"Tell me, how are things in Poland? How are the people getting on? Have you been in Lublin? How are things in Warsaw?" I inundated them with questions.

They did not want to talk to me at first, but after I pressed them for a time I discovered a few things that sent a chill down my spine. "Don't tell strangers that before the war you were in prison for being a Communist. Haven't you heard about the gangs? There is no peace in Poland. People are dying every day. Be careful," one of them shouted when they jumped off the car at a station. We traveled further, all the way to Bydgoszcz.* When I saw the large sign on the Bydgoszcz station, I decided to get off.

We wandered around the tracks. We had a loaf of bread in our bag, which had been given to us by the Polish soldiers. There was no need for us to hurry. There were a lot of people milling around the station with huge packages and valises. Where had they come from, and where were they going? I did not have the nerve to ask. I had heard nothing about these expeditions to the west to pick up the goods that had been left behind by the Germans. A train pulled into the station filled with soldiers who had no belts and no weapons. "Those are deserters," someone told me. I had gone no farther than Bydgoszcz, and already my bubble had burst, my dream that if I could just get to Poland everything would be alright. I had imagined that they would be waiting for us, the political prisoners and the prisoners from the concentration camps, with flowers. Instead we wandered around the station, hungry and dirty, and nobody paid any attention to us. Maybe it was better this way, I thought, remembering the parting words of the soldiers.

After lunch a civilian train pulled in. The older lady and her daughter did not want to go any farther. I did not think much about it. I got on the train and let myself into a compartment. I even found a spot near a window. I looked eagerly at the passing villages and towns, so homey and so close to my heart. I was so taken with the scenery that I did not hear the conductor when he asked, "Ticket, please?" What was he saying? I was very surprised. Did he want a ticket from me, a visitor from another planet? Did he not realize where I had been? "I don't have a ticket," I shouted angrily. "Where would I get money to buy it with? They didn't give us money in the German camp."

"Excuse me, I didn't know," he said gently.

Now I really became interested in the train's destination. "Please, sir, can you tell me where this train is headed?"

"You don't know? This train is going to Lodz."

"Can I get a train from Lodz to Lublin?" I asked.

---

*Bydgoszcz is the capital of Bydgoszcz Province in north central Poland. The city had a Jewish populace of about 3,000 before World War II.

"There are no passenger trains to Lublin as yet, but there is a freight train. Some of the freight cars are set aside for passengers."

I had found out what I had to know. I relaxed now and enjoyed the scenery. As the train came closer to my home, my anxiety increased. What was waiting for me? I had already cried for the death of my whole family in April 1942. But would I be able to look quietly at the house and the city where my parents, my brother, my sister-in-law, and all my relatives had died so tragically?

"Please, lady." Someone's voice tore me from my thoughts. The conductor was standing in front of me. "I brought you something to eat. Please accept it. It's Polish food," he added, seeing my confusion. There were two pieces of fresh white bread thickly spread with lard. In the thermos he had some hot tea. I ate. He did not ask questions, for which I was grateful. I did not have the strength to talk, right now, just to satisfy someone's curiosity. The past and present were getting mixed up in my whirling head. Nothing seemed real to me. Later that evening I arrived in Lodz. The station was filled with people. Every inch of the walkway was occupied by people, standing, or else sitting on packages and valises, or simply sitting right on the floor. I sat down near the tracks. All around me people were shouting to each other, telling each other stories, laughing and eating. I listened, but the words did not make any sense to me. I was asked a question about something, but I did not answer. I simply could not speak. I was really very sick from what I had lived through the last few weeks. Everybody around me was waiting for the same train that I was. The train was to arrive at approximately ten o'clock in the morning. I spent the whole night sitting on the walkway. Very early in the morning everybody started getting ready to fight for a place on the train. At a little before ten, two civilians came with red armbands on their sleeves and carrying carbines on their shoulders. The train had not yet arrived, but the armed civilians stood in line waiting for it. I noticed that only those who pushed money into the hands of the armed personnel had a chance of getting on the train. Anyone without money was unceremoniously shunted aside. I was afraid to get stuck among those hags with packages. I imagined that they would trample me without giving it a thought.

At ten o'clock a long freight train arrived. They opened the large doors of a few of the cars, and the people, together with their packages, started pushing toward the entrance. The two caretakers with the carbines shuffled along with the passengers. "It's full," screamed one of the hags. "Lady, shut the door. Nobody else can fit in here." The door was closed. Then I stepped up to one of the armed men.

"Mister," I uttered in despair, "I don't have any money. I am returning from the camp. You see, sir,"—I showed him the number tattooed on my arm—"I have a new sheet. I will give it to you. Please let me get on the train." I took the sheet from my bag. He took it. He opened the door and threw me in at the last minute. The train started.

I sat on the floor, in the middle of the car. It was quite dark in there, because the only light came from two little windows near the ceiling. As usual, the passengers in the car divided into several groups. They treated my intrusion with complete indifference. They spread out napkins before themselves and started to eat. Here and there a bottle of whisky appeared.

There was a bench under the windows and a group formed there. A few women and men were listening with bated breath to a story being told by a young man in an old worn-out army officer's cap from which the eagle had been torn. "I'm telling you"— I kept overhearing scraps of his story—"when I saw Russian officers in the Polish army, I thought to myself, this is not for you. Run away from this army. They'll never live to see the day that I fight for a Communist Poland. I took off, and you see how they shot at me and almost killed me. I took care of a few of them on the way, though. I have a gun. It will come in handy against the Reds."

"Drink, you poor soul." One woman became very mushy about the whole thing and put a glass of whisky in his hand. A second woman gave him bread, salami, and an egg without a shell. He removed his cap and it was then that I saw that his head was bandaged with a bloody rag.

"What do you think," somebody said in another corner of the car, "that things will stay the way they are now? Nothing doing! The Soviets will never lord it over us. You'll see. Anders will come back from London and chase those beggars the hell out of here."

"What are you carrying?" another woman asked.

"Men's shirts and materials from the warehouse in Szczecin. I bought the stuff from somebody who somehow sneaked into the warehouse."

As I listened to these conversations my skin crawled. I lowered my head and pretended to be asleep. I was scared. I was trying to think of what I could tell them when they got around to asking me where I came from. Could I admit to these people that I had just come from the camp? They could strangle me in this terrible car if they found out that I am a Red. If only I could hold out until night time, then it would be easier to hide in a corner. I was very hungry, and I had nothing to eat with me. No one offered me even a crumb of bread, even though they had everything and were eating all they wanted.

Soon the car was enveloped in total darkness. Everyone went to sleep. I fell asleep, too.

Early the next morning they all started arranging their packages, dividing them into smaller packages, so that they would not be conspicuous.

"Lady, you don't have any baggage. Maybe you can take one of my valises," one of the women said to me.

"I can't. I am sick," I answered.

At twelve noon the doors suddenly slid open. We were in Lublin. I was the first one to leave. As I reached the street, I was greeted by a colorful Easter procession. There was a colorful crowd of women dressed in their native costumes, children, and elegant men. There was no room on the street. All of the balconies and windows were decorated with rugs, flowers, and pictures of the Holy Family.

So this is Poland. I understood the words of the Polish soldiers whom I met on the border: "Don't tell the people you meet that you are a Communist." The fight had not ended. A fight takes time.

EDITORS' AFTERWORD

he Holocaust left a legacy of fundamental questions that touch the core of human existence as it is reflected in Western, and primarily Christian, civilization, questions of God's silence and of the indifference of those who professed to believe in a faith that affirmed the dignity of all human beings. Out of the ruins has emerged a bizarre tale, awesome in its irony—a tale worth telling and telling again. It is a story about the telling of a story, in fact about the telling of six million stories, or maybe six million tellings of one story of the implementation of a demonic design, the all-out effort of a technologically advanced civilization to first dehumanize and then exterminate an entire people. The story of the telling of the tale concerns tellers young and old, scholars and craftsmen, who, charged with a sacred sense of mission, sought to preserve the Jewish memory and to uphold the humanness of the victims in the face of an ingenious SS machine designed to strip them of their individuality and turn them into ciphers crammed into concentration-camp logbooks.

In the walled-in ghettos, behind the barbed wires of the concentration camps, on the bloody trails in the woods, and in stifling hideouts, the persecuted took time out from their bread reveries and snatched minutes from their nightmares to put down what their eyes had witnessed, what their hearts had felt, and what their minds had pondered. Gazing at these pages written in a babel of languages, one wonders what it was that motivated these obsessed witness bearers. Was it the instinctive response of an organism to the threat of extinction, or was it a manifestation of a collective consciousness rooted in a long tradition and guided by a historic imperative to remember and remind? A hint of an answer to these questions may be found in the following talmudic tale.[1]

In the year 70 A.D., as Jerusalem was under siege, surrounded by the Roman legions commanded by Vespasian, a passionate de-

1. Gittin 56 A and B, *The Babylonian Talmud* (London: The Soncino Press, 1960).

bate took place inside the walls as to whether they should come to terms with the enemy or keep on fighting. Rabban Yohanan Ben Zakkai, a recognized spiritual leader, counseled moderation. Since the Jews could not possibly defeat the mighty Roman legions, they should seek some accommodation. Subsequently, Yohanan managed to escape from the city. On reaching the Roman lines, the story goes, he encountered Vespasian, the Roman general, whom he hailed as follows: "Peace to you, O King, Peace to you, O King!" Rabban Yohanan's greetings, we are told, turned out to be prophetic. For even as Vespasian was objecting to the bestowed title of king, a messenger arrived from Rome announcing: "The Emperor is dead, and the notables of Rome have chosen you Head of State." As an expression of gratitude for his prophetic utterances, Vespasian granted Yohanan one request.

One might well expect that Yohanan would have asked for the release of his family, still under siege, or for the sacred religious relics and treasures lying in the temple. Instead, the request that Yohanan put to the newly appointed emperor was as laconic as it was portentous: "Give me Yavneh and its scholars."

At this momentous juncture in Jewish history, Yohanan set his eyes on the future. It was phenomenal foresight. In deciding to save Yavneh, Yohanan saved the Jewish heritage from extinction. The words of the Torah that came from the school of Yavneh stimulated an impulse for the evolution of rituals and ceremonies exhorting the Jewish people to preserve the past in memory. As a consequence, it became possible, following the destruction of the Second Temple, to absorb the grief of the people and to convert it into a vehicle for spiritual renewal during the long period of exile.

Approximately 1900 years later in a continent far away from the land of Israel, the collective Jewish memory was again put to the test. In the shadow of the Nazi swastika, a contest was taking place between the perpetrator, who was determined to erase the memory of an entire people from the collective consciousness of mankind, and the persecuted, who were equally resolved to foil the oppressor, not necessarily by escaping personal extinction but by keeping and concealing historical records for the information of future generations, even when individual survival had clearly become impossible. Following in the footsteps of the biblical and talmudic tradition, the designated victims resorted to an unprecedented recording of their experiences. Ultimately, recording becomes synonymous with remembering and remembering with spiritual resistance. This three-stranded, braided cable of recording, remembering, and resisting is the quintessence of the following message delivered by Rabbi Nachum Yanchiker to his students at the Slabodka-Musar Yeshiva in the fateful year 1941:

My dear students, when the world returns again to stability and quiet, never become tired of teaching the glories, the wisdom, the Torah and the Musar of Lithuania, the beautiful life which Jews lived here. Do not become embittered by wailing and tears. Speak of these matters with calmness and serenity, as did our Holy Sages in the Midrash, "LAMENTIONS RABBATI." And do as our Holy Sages have done—pour forth your words and cast them into letters. This will be the greatest retribution which you can wreak on the wicked ones. Despite the raging wrath of our foes, the holy souls of your brothers and sisters will then remain alive. These evil ones schemed to blot out their names from the face of the earth; but a man cannot destroy letters. For words have wings; they mount heavenly heights and they endure for eternity.[2]

As though she had been one of those students addressed by Rabbi Yanchiker, Sara Nomberg-Przytyk stored her Holocaust experiences in memory, and when the world returned to relative stability and quiet, she began to speak of these matters with calmness and serenity, and, for the most part, without bitterness and wailing. It is one of the still unresolved problems of that body of writings called Holocaust literature that the events seem to overwhelm all attempts to impose formal order, either of literary history or literary criticism. The problem of ordering, categorizing, and interpreting is further exacerbated by the perverse efforts of

2. Rabbi Nachum Yanchiker, *Forms of Prayer for Jewish Worship*, ed. The Assembly of Rabbis of the Reform Synagogues of Great Britain (London and Oxford: Oxford University Press, 1977), pp. 256–57.

so-called revisionist historians who deny everything, deny that the Nazis exterminated millions of Jews and others, thereby placing an additional burden on those who wish to study the ways in which imagination modifies memory and fiction vitalizes history.

Among witnessing authors, Elie Wiesel is preeminent for his poetic and novelistic evocation of the death-camp experience. No one has labored more assiduously to reveal the multi-faceted reality of survivorship. Yet even Wiesel has recognized that sometimes it is only fiction that can make the truth credible, just as it is only imagination that can make memory tolerable. This vision is expressed in a dialogue between Wiesel and a *rebbe*, as reported in the introduction to *Legends of Our Time*:

"What are you writing?" the Rebbe asked. "Stories," I said. He wanted to know what kind of stories. "True stories." "About people you knew?" "Yes, about people I might have known." "About things that happened?" "Yes, about things that happened or could have happened." "But they did not?" "No, not all of them did. In fact, some were invented from almost the beginning to almost the end." The Rebbe leaned forward as if to measure me up and said with more sorrow than anger: "That means you are writing lies!" I did not answer immediately. The scolded child within me had nothing to say in his defense. Yet, I had to justify myself: "Things are not that simple, Rebbe. Some events do take place but are not true; others are, although they never occurred."[3]

In reporting his conversation with the *rebbe*, Wiesel has pinpointed one of the major problems faced by witnessing authors in writing about the Holocaust. To tell the story as it "happened," as unembellished, unadulterated "realism," would strain the reader's credulity, for the concentration-camp world was stripped of the basic premises constituting a normative society. The cause and effect link, for example, that defines our relationship to our surroundings was rendered inoperative in the concentration-

3. Elie Wiesel, *Legends of Our Time* (New York: Holt, Rinehart and Winston, 1968), p. viii.

camp environment. The relative freedom that enabled a person to arrange his life within a causal context was brutally denied to the concentration-camp inmate. Consequently, the inmate was deprived of the psychological props indispensable to the individual in orienting himself to the world. Paradoxically, a swing to "pure" imagination would be equally inadequate, for to cast the camp reality into wholly metaphoric structures would undermine the historicity of the events. Since the relatedness of memory and imagination has only been touched upon with regard to Holocaust narratives, critics have not recognized that neither can be relied on as an absolute constant. Both are variables. The challenge to the witnessing author, therefore, is to use traditional mimetic forms to convert the repugnant, intolerable reality he witnessed into an intimation of reality that can be both accepted and tolerated by a sensitive, normatively oriented reader.

The credibility factor occupied the chronicler under siege as far back as 1941. Fearing that the depositions of victims in the Warsaw Ghetto would be received with skepticism after the war, Emmanuel Ringelblum instructed his chroniclers to adhere strictly to bare facts and to avoid emotional coloring in their reports. "Comprehensiveness was the chief principle guiding our work," notes Ringelblum in his diary, "and objectivity was the second principle guiding our work. We aspired to tell the whole truth, however painful it may be."[4]

About the same time, in the Lodz Ghetto, a high school boy by the name of S. Dratwa envisioned how producers would make a film of the Jewish tragedy after the war, predicting, at the same time, the kind of response the film would elicit from the audience. In his mind's eye, he saw the audience watching the film:

> *Wrapt in emotion,*
> *Quivering with pleasure,*
> *Everyone will think:*
> *"The film is fabulous,*

---

4. Emmanuel Ringelblum, *Notes from the Warsaw Ghetto*, ed. and trans. Jacob Sloan (New York: Schocken Books, 1958).

The scenes are wonderful,
But nothing is true.

They are only tales from a grotesque land.[5]

Unwittingly the young Dratwa posited the crucial question of how to portray a grotesque world and yet make it seem historically true. What the besieged Dratwa foresaw, Elie Wiesel survived to see, and having seen it, he has tried to caution the world against converting a historical event of immeasurable human pain into a merely grotesque fiction divested of its historic dimension.

Like Wiesel, Sara survived to draw her disturbing vignettes, and in drawing them to make the grotesque reality believable. She is a natural storyteller who has the capacity to render the unbearable tolerable by suffusing her narrative with a radiance of imagination, treading a fine line between history and fiction, between document and novel. The present editors and others who have read her "stories" have been startled by her ability to convey the most depressing materials without depressing the reader. She does this, we believe, with the skill of the novelist, creating the illusion of vibrant life and the will to live even in the kingdom of death, making her characters live in the reader's imagination. And she accomplishes this feat with utmost economy in her brief vignettes.

Sara's interest in character, however, is not Dostoyevskyan in nature. Rather, her characters exist as constituents of the death-camp reality. Though the individuals whom Sara recalls are often fascinating in themselves, each one is, nevertheless, anchored to a camp happening; consequently, it is the aggregate of the individual vignettes that structures the incarnation of the actual camp experience.

As an example of Sara's storytelling art we would like to examine briefly the vignette entitled "Old Words—New Meanings," which can be perceived as being in some sense a microcosm of the book as a whole. On casual reading, the vignette appears to be

---

5. S. Dratwa, "A Jewish Grave," trans. Eli Pfefferkorn and Mark Goldman, *Midstream*, Vol. XXX, No. 4, p. 39. From the Katznelson Museum Archive.

a simple, plainly told story of the young girl Fela. In telling Fela's story, Sara exposes some of the grimmest aspects of camp life: sick, starving prisoners who must cheat each other to stay alive— an economy in which every scrap of bread one eats is life-bread taken from someone else, and not only is this the case but everyone who has a crust of bread *knows* this is the case; *kanada,* the gruesomely conceived warehouse storing belongings of the dead and those consigned to death; and finally, "selection" and the gas, the insane process by which people are more or less randomly inscribed for life or death by Dr. Mengele and his cohorts.

It is our impression, confirmed by other readers, that the horrors are not immediately perceived as such by the reader because of Sara's narrative technique. She begins her story with a more or less abstract concept: the collapse of normative reality in the camps, which results in a corresponding disfiguration of language and a change in alignment between sound images and the concepts to which they refer. Specifically the word "organize," a signifier normally associated with social order and well-being, has come to denote the activities involved in procuring the basic elements necessary to sustain physical existence.

Sara writes in the tradition of the Yiddish folktale. Though her stories are simply told, they stimulate the reader to contemplate complex issues that belie the apparent simplicity of the surface structure. Hence, in the tale at hand, she quickly roots the abstract notion of a collapse of reality reflected in a collapse of normative linguistic usage in the story of Fela, a young girl who learns not only the new meaning of the *word* "organize" but also learns *how* to "organize," i.e. who becomes a master of the new reality. It is, of course, the reader's consequent fascination with the character of Fela that pushes the ghastly aspects of camp life into the background, where they register on the subliminal consciousness. Consider, for example, Sara's brief description of Fela and her situation: "Eighteen years old . . . she had been sent to Auschwitz when she was caught smuggling food into the ghetto for her family. She was a tall, slim girl with very light blond hair. She was not a beauty, but she had a quality that was impossible to describe. Something forced you to look at her. She was alone, without family or friends, but in spite of that, she did not give the impression of being helpless."

Though the sketch is drawn in a few brief sentences, the reader has already learned much about Fela. From the fact that she was caught smuggling food into the ghetto for her family, we may infer that she was courageous, resourceful, devoted, and not simply looking out for herself. We also learn something about the abhorrent conditions of ghetto life, where people were left to starve unless they engaged in the activity of illegal barter and two-way smuggling (the smuggling of valuables out of the ghetto and food back in). Avoiding the possible pathos of labeling Fela as "a beauty," Sara nevertheless conveys an image of Fela's physical attractiveness. She further engages the reader's sympathy by writing that Fela "was alone," revealing that the family for whom she had risked her life by smuggling had been exterminated. In conveying this information indirectly, Sara does not permit us to dwell on the depressing horrors but forces us, rather, to focus on the intriguing figure of Fela herself, and she arouses the reader's interest further with the statement "she did not give the impression of being helpless." We now wait to see how Fela is going to help herself in this destructive environment, how she is going to "organize." Against the drab and depressing facts of life under Nazi occupation, the colorful image of Fela emerges to pique the reader's curiosity and to overpower the dominance of concentration-camp gray.

Having set up this image, the narrator re-introduces herself as a reflector rather than a character. She registers a traditional value system superseded by the quasi-Darwinian camp ethic of survival of the most ruthless. The young Fela, on the other hand, seems to have made the necessary adjustment to the new value system. In a social order that allows only two classes—victims and victimizers, and nothing between—she is determined not to be one of the victims, even though it means abandoning all scruples. When Fela concludes her cynical outburst by saying, "I have to organize something," Sara comments that this is the first time she has heard the word "in the new Auschwitz sense." Since the word itself was commonplace in the camp, one might suspect the precise accuracy of Sara's memory here; nevertheless, one would not have it otherwise since dramatic truth here takes precedence over factual precision.

When Sara next meets Fela, the young woman is carrying a sack full of bread, certainly a most unusual occurrence in Auschwitz. Sara immediately suspects that Fela has stolen bread from the sick and accuses her, whereupon Fela, who is apparently not fully hardened, explains that she not only did not steal the bread but earned it by performing a service for the sick women, giving them her home-cooked potato soup in return for their hard, crusty bread, which they cannot chew anyway. In the course of recounting Fela's explanation, Sara provides the reader with a vivid account of the economy of camp life. Bread is bartered for potatoes and onions, which are then cooked into potato soup that is traded for more bread, which in sufficient quantity can be traded for cigarettes. The cigarettes can then be used to buy all other commodities and can even improve one's work assignment when used to bribe the officials.

In the face of Fela's entrepreneurial genius, Sara perceives a moral and ethical dilemma. Compared to the general camp regimen, Fela's bartering, though "ugly," is relatively harmless and perhaps even beneficial: "I stood there facing her, not knowing what to say to her or how to act toward her. It was certainly an ugly way of 'earning' bread, taking it from unfortunate, very sick women, tearing the very last bite out of their mouths. But that is what they wanted. They preferred this cup of watery soup smelling of home to the portion of stale bread. To throw Fela out of the hospital would be to deprive the women of the soup for which they had been waiting all day. Nobody else would 'organize' the soup."

In an evil kingdom in which only successful predators are permitted to exist, Fela is at least a benign predator. By Auschwitz standards Fela has earned an A+ in morality. But what is her grade when seen in a larger perspective? Dare one assign such a grade?

The next time Sara encounters Fela, the latter has achieved her goal. She has "organized" a job in *kanada* (presumably by parlaying her bread and cigarettes), where a prisoner can acquire some of the creature comforts that are left behind by the dying and the dead. One striking sentence stands out in the narrator's description of the *kanada komando*: "They wore red kerchiefs on their heads and belts that were made especially to each girl's measurements." The color associated with Fela, a flash of bright red, leaps boldly out of the gray Auschwitz background, as does Fela's pride, for she has no qualms about waving her red kerchief to attract Sara's attention.

It turns out, however, that Fela's "organizing" abilities are no match for the cruelties of Auschwitz. She leaves the *kanada komando* because she is shaken by the sight of the bodies of children who have died of asphyxiation as a result of having been packed in valises by parents who hoped to save them. Nor can she take any pleasure in the garments and baubles that once belonged to the dead. These fundamental details of the death-factory warehouse, including the valises that became coffins for dead children, have been told before but rarely with Sara's ability to subordinate them to the dramatic existence of individual characters.

It is through this subordinating of the horrors to the individual characters that Sara moves from documentarian to novelist, and it is as a novelist that she heightens the reader's awareness of the complexity of the moral and ethical problems posed by Auschwitz. Fela is a decent person. She has cared for her family, not only in the "normal" past but even in the murderous ghetto environment, which was not much better than that of the camps. Finding herself a lone survivor in Auschwitz, she resolves to survive at any price. Yet, even in her survivalist desperation, she finds a method of "organizing" that is morally ambiguous at worst. She takes bread from sick women but gives them something in return. Her "organizing" of a job in *kanada* is a further step toward degradation; she does not directly inflict physical injury but lives like a vulture off carrion. But apparently, she is too sensitive to remain in this environment and must plunge back into greater physical danger for the sake of psychological or spiritual survival.

At this point one might expect the story to end. But with the touch of the master storyteller, Sara adds a coda, using, with great effectiveness, a traditional folktale device that she uses elsewhere in the narrative, the tale within a tale. We seem to shift from Fela momentarily as Sara starts to describe an "interlude" in the killing. It is, of course, not really an interlude, since the guests at the little gathering in the infirmary belong to the *leichenkomando*, the detail assigned to dispose of the corpses. At this point, the SS driver of the *leichenauto* deposits a soot-covered bundle which turns out to be Fela, at the infirmary. Now Fela completes her story in her own words, a story of symbolic death and resurrection (the SS man who permits her to live apparently thinks she is "a creature not of this earth"). Once again Fela has saved herself; this time, however, not at anyone's expense but by quick thinking, some risk-taking, and good luck. Having been selected by Dr. Mengele, she avoids the gas by leaping down the chimney of a car that could be powered by burning wood or petroleum. As she tells the story in her own words, the reader cannot help but sympathize with her plight and rejoice at her survival, at the same time being aware of the tragedy of those who were not so resourceful or fortunate.

From Sara's dramatization one more intriguing question emerges: Why did the SS man who found Fela the next morning not finish her off? Why did he go to the trouble of delivering her to the infirmary, where she might (and did) find at least a temporary haven? Given the SS ideology and given the fact that the SS driver had just participated in mass murder the night before, how can one explain this human behavior on the part of a trained mass killer? Is it that once Fela had separated herself from the others the SS man had to deal with her as an individual? Or is it that once the death machine was temporarily closed down, there was no point in gratuitous killing until it was started up again? When the death machine was at rest, so was this one small cog.

It is fitting that the story of Fela should remain open-ended. As Sara tells it: "She left Auschwitz with the next transport. I do not know whether she 'organized' further. I never saw her again."

Sara's narrative is replete with such dramatizations. For example, a frequently described ghastly phenomenon was the SS ban on women's giving birth in the camp and the subsequent decision by Jewish camp medical personnel to kill the new-born infants in the hope of saving the lives of the mothers. (For a first-hand factual account see Olga Lengyel, *Five Chimneys*).[6] Sara, once again, presents the horrifying fact "novelistically" in her touching portrait of the naïve Esther, who has no way of comprehending the sadism of the pathologically murderous Mengele.

Sara's ability to walk the fine line between memory and imagination, document and fiction, opens up new perspectives on Holocaust literature. There are several thoughtful studies of this literature, but they are incomplete and to a large extent uncertain of the direction they wish to take. The authors seem to be confused as to whether they should be concerned with "high art" or with factual accuracy, whether to deal with the historical event or with the representations of the event. Lawrence L. Langer, for example, chooses to pursue the elitist course in his first book, *The Holocaust and the Literary Imagination*, searching out instances of literary excellence and analyzing them only in terms of the high standards of the New Criticism. But in his recent *Versions of Survival* he moves into an almost exclusive concern with Holocaust literature as document, focusing on accuracy, and sitting in moral judgment. Alvin Rosenfeld, in *A Double Dying*, stresses the fact that old forms and traditional tropes are no longer available to Holocaust writers but concentrates, nevertheless, on works that use the old forms and the traditional tropes. Terrence Des Pres, on the other hand, provides a fine taxonomy of documentary narratives, condensing descriptions of both the strategies for survival and the conditions under which the prisoners lived, but he shows little interest in narrative and poetic method.[7] Sara's narra-

6. Olga Lengyel, *Five Chimneys* (Chicago and New York: Ziff-Davis Publishing Company, 1947), pp. 99–103.
7. Terrence Des Pres, *The Survivor: An Anatomy of Life in the Death Camps* (New York: Oxford University Press, 1976); Lawrence L. Langer, *The Holocaust and the Literary Imagination* (New Haven and London: Yale University Press, 1975) and *Versions of Survival: The Holocaust and the Human Spirit* (Albany, New York: SUNY Press, 1982); Alvin Rosenfeld, *A Double Dying: Reflections on Holocaust Literature* (Bloomington: Indiana University Press, 1980).

tive forces us to develop a dual focus that embraces both the actualities of camp life and the artistry with which those actualities are represented. In forcing this dual focus upon us, Sara's narrative may also point us toward a much-needed morphology of camp narratives. Although Des Pres comes close to providing such a morphology, he falls short because he is more interested in the psychology of surviving than in the strategies survivors employed to convey behavior too cruel and bizarre, suffering too prolonged and intense to be believed by an audience that knows only the conventional cruelty common to normative social systems.

In the space available here we shall attempt only the barest outlines of such a morphology. One must begin with certain patterns of social organization that were so commonplace to camp life, yet so unusual in civilized society, that they are described in every documentary account and in many of the impressionistic accounts. So brutal and inhuman were these patterns that many of them have become common knowledge, even among those who do not take a special interest in Nazi atrocities. For example, the transport of innocent men, women, and children in crowded cattle cars, without food, water, or even air is fairly generally known. Other commonplace features of camp life that often turn up in Auschwitz narratives are: arrival on the gravel-strewn ramp, roll call, dysentery, selections, lice, "organizing," "*kanada*," the watery camp "soup." As indicated, Sara dramatizes these phenomena instead of merely describing them.

In contrast to these constant, day-in-day-out tortures of hunger, thirst, filth, lice, dysentery, beatings, and other afflictions, there were certain occurrences in the concentration camps that were strikingly dramatic and were recorded both for their inherent dramatic quality and for their divergence from the gray, dreary diurnal existence of the camp routine. These occurrences were sometimes individual acts of defiance, and sometimes they were mass acts. Perhaps the best known of the former variety is the frequently discussed incident in which a naked woman on her way to the gas disarms an SS man, shoots him down with his own gun, and then is shot in turn, thus avoiding the degradation of mass execution. Bruno Bettelheim made this story famous by adapting Eugen Kogon's telling of it. In Kogon's version, told in three brief sentences, an Italian dancer is ordered by the SS *rapportführer* Schillinger to dance naked in front of him before going to the gas. She manages to get close enough to him to grab his pistol and shoot him. Kogon ends the account with: "In the ensuing struggle, the woman herself was shot, thus at least avoiding death by gassing."[8]

Bettelheim speculated that the act of dancing, of practicing her "vocation," may have "made her once again a person. Transformed, however momentarily, she responded like her old self, destroying the enemy bent on her destruction, even if she had to die in the process."[9] Bettelheim's use of this incident as a possible paradigm of prisoner behavior and as a cudgel to use on other prisoners who did not do what the "Italian dancer" did has resulted in extensive controversy that we cannot enter into here.[10] Suffice it to say that Kogon does not cite the source of his information, and since the incident took place in the crematorium, it could have been witnessed only by the SS, the *sonderkommando*, and those who died in the gas chambers.

Tadeusz Borowski tells the story somewhat differently—at greater length and more "artfully." He creates narrative distance by presenting the incident as a story told to him by a friend who was foreman of the *sonderkommando* and who was a witness to the event. In Borowski's story within a story, the woman who shot SS man Schillinger in the "cremo" was not an Italian dancer but an "ordinary" Polish Jewess. As the witnessing foreman had put it

8. Eugen Kogon, *Der SS-Staat* (Stockholm, Sweden: Bermann-Fischer Verlag AB, 1947), p. 180.
9. Bruno Bettelheim, *The Informed Heart: Autonomy in a Mass Age* (New York: The Free Press of Glencoe, Inc., 1960), pp. 264–65.
10. See Eli Pfefferkorn, "Bettelheim, Wertmuller, and the Morality of Survival," *Post Script*, 1 (Winter, 1982): 15–26; "The Case of Bruno Bettelheim and Lina Wertmuller's *Seven Beauties*," *The Nazi Concentration Camps* (Jerusalem: Yad Vashem, 1984), pp. 663–81. Basically, the controversy centers around Bettelheim's contention that those who had the best chance of surviving in the camps were prisoners who were able to set up sophisticated psychological defenses and to find strategies for retaining old human values in the new hostile environment.

to the Borowski narrator, "Our Polish Jews knew what was up." The foreman then describes how, when Schillinger grabbed the woman's arm, "the naked woman bent down suddenly, scooped a handful of gravel and threw it in his face, and when Schillinger cried out in pain and dropped his revolver, the woman snatched it up and fired several shots into his abdomen."[11] In Borowski's account it is toughness, savvy, and desperation that count. Moreover, Borowski's use of irony, a common feature of Polish works of fiction, gives his story an appearance of fiction even though he was in a better position than Kogon to get the facts straight. The irony lies in Borowski's report of the brutal Schillinger's whining complaint after being shot: "O God, my God, what have I done to deserve such suffering?" As Borowski tells the story there is no basis for Bettelheim's speculations, and he ends his story with an anticlimactic and dampening description of a well-known historical incident, the revolt of the *sonderkomando* in the crematorium.

Wieslaw Kielar, in his powerful Auschwitz narrative, *Anus Mundi*, tells the story in a way that is close to, but not identical with, Borowski's telling. Kielar does not specify the woman's nationality or occupation, but he describes her as "beautiful." According to the Kielar version, as Schillinger tried to pull down the woman's brassiere, she grabbed his gun and shot him in the struggle. Like Borowski, Kielar follows this account with some mention of the revolt of the *sonderkomando*, but he draws much different conclusions from the woman's act. "The incident," he says, "passed on from mouth to mouth and embellished in various ways grew into a legend. Without doubt this heroic deed by a weak woman, in the face of certain death, gave moral support to every prisoner."[12]

Sara tells a similar story with a slightly different setting and with a different cast of characters. Like Borowski, she represents

11. Tadeusz Borowski, "The Death of Schillinger," in *This Way for the Gas, Ladies and Gentlemen*, trans. Barbara Vedder (New York: Penguin Books, 1982), pp. 143–46. First published in Poland in 1959 and in the United States by Viking in 1967.
12. Wieslaw Kielar, *Anus Mundi*, translated from the German by Susanne Flatauer (New York: Times Books, 1980), pp. 177–79.

herself as retelling a tale that has been told to her. In her version, the woman is a French dancer, but the incident takes place on the unloading platform instead of in the crematorium. In Sara's narrative, the woman is the only one in this transport who refuses to undress. When an unidentified SS man approaches her to get her to remove the bathing suit she has been wearing on the trip, she grabs the pistol out of his holster and shoots him.[13] It may be, of course, that Sara's story is of another incident that is similar to the three just mentioned. But Sara's variant presents a fully coherent dramatic action, setting the moral implications into sharp focus. Here, the woman's behavior is an unambiguous act of defiance and a conscious assertion of her human dignity. By saving the last bullet for herself, she cheats the dehumanizing death apparatus. The narrator wisely draws no moral at this point, simply leaving the reader to ponder Magda's comment, "That's how you're supposed to die." Once again, it should be noted, we have an instance of inexplicable behavior by the oppressor, an act of kindness by a German soldier which saves the young French girl, thus permitting her to relate the incident to Sara, who then tells it to us.

Of the inherently dramatic "public events" that are often told, none has been more widely disseminated than the romance of Mala and Edek (Tadeusz in Sara's version). This romance, a Romeo and Juliet story, as Sara correctly points out, exists in at least five versions. Those who are interested in comparing them point by point should, of course, read all five. We shall point out only a few of the differences among the various versions.[14] Seweryna Szmaglewska gives the girl's name as Zimmerman, while Kielar gives it as Zimetbaum. Fania Fenelon writes that the girl was an interpreter, the others that she was a *läuferin* or *lauferka* (messenger or runner). Sara and Fania agree that she was Belgian; Lengyel thinks she was a Jewish Pole and Kielar that she was a

---

13. "Revenge of a Dancer."
14. The tellings alluded to here occur in: Fania Fenelon, *Playing for Time* (New York: Athenaeum, 1977), pp. 157–68; Kielar, *Anus Mundi*, pp. 215–55 and passim; Lengyel, *Five Chimneys*, pp. 124–25; Seweryna Szmaglewska, *Smoke Over Birkenau*, trans. Jadwiga Rynas (New York: Henry Holt and Company, 1947), p. 296.

Slovak Jewess, though this is less apparent in the English translation. The descriptions of the executions are similar, yet they differ
in minor details. All agree that Mala slapped someone and that
she remained defiant to the end, refusing to die the death that the
SS had planned for her.

Of greater significance is the portrayal of Mala and Edek as
individuals. The accounts of Szmaglewska and Lengyel are insig-
nificant in this respect, simply recounting the bare events. Fania
and Sara, however, knew Mala and portray her as an extraordinary heroine—brilliant, courageous, and strong. Kielar, who was
supposed to escape with Edek and Mala, and who describes himself as a close friend of Edek's, portrays Mala a little less glori-
ously, although he portrays Edek as being, in sharp contrast to
himself, noble and heroic. Mala, in Kielar's portrait, emerges as a
vulnerable woman who achieves her heroism at the gallows. Perhaps the most important fact is that all accounts agree that the
love between Mala and Edek was remarkable, a deep and unselfish affection that could flourish even in the cauldron of hate that
was Auschwitz-Birkenau.[15] With her unerring dramatic sense,
Sara weaves this tale and its moral into a powerful, compact vignette that brings the dying lovers together as a symbol of the
triumph of love over tyranny and death.

A quite different kind of public event that has also been widely
described and that has shocked even those inured to the death
machinery of Auschwitz was the extermination of the gypsy camp.
Unlike the incident of the dancer or of Mala and Edek, this was
a mass event of cataclysmic proportions. The gypsies had been
lulled into a false sense of security by being set up in a family
camp. All of the prisoners, including the gypsies themselves, took
this as a sign that the SS planned to use them mainly as forced
labor. On a single night in either August or October, 1944 (ac-

15. There is an unfortunate mistranslation of a sentence in the original Polish that
underscores Edek's devotion and loyalty to Mala. In the English version of Kielar's
account, p. 227, Edek tells the narrator: "You must understand me. I have no
obligation to Mala." The Polish clearly states the reverse. Edek says, "You must
understand me. I have an obligation to Mala."

counts differ), the entire remnants of the gypsy family camp were liquidated. It has been estimated that from the first shipment of gypsies on 26 February 1943, a total of almost 22,000 gypsies were sent to Auschwitz and that by 1 August 1944, 15,000 had been murdered. Estimates vary on the number killed the night the gypsy camp was liquidated. Sara's estimate of 25,000 is high, and what she appears to have in mind is the total number of gypsies killed in Auschwitz over a period of twenty months. Miklos Nyiszli puts the number killed that one night at 4,500, and Danuta Czech puts it at 2,897.[16] For some reason, all of those who tell of this catastrophic night seem to remember the sound of the engines. As is her wont, Sara's narrative genius instinctively leads her to connect the incomprehensible mass slaughter to the devastating tale of the gypsy boy who was, as the *sonderkomando* later tells her, pushed into the gas chamber by Mengele himself (note the parallels between this story and the incident of "Mandel and the Child" told by Fania Fenelon). Perhaps we should not try to add anything to Sara's chilling narrative of the gypsy boy. We wish simply to reinforce Sara's genius for getting at the deeper truth of these terrible concentration-camp events by recording here a song that Aleksander Kulisiewicz tells us was written by a Cracow student, Roman Friedlein, for a little gypsy girl dancing behind the wires of the gypsy camp. By performing the dance, Kulisiewicz tells us, the girl was begging for bread. The author himself was dying of tuberculosis in the "hospital" at Birkenau and witnessed the gassing of the gypsies shortly before he died:

> *I don't have anybody.*
> *I spit blood in my filthy bunk.*
> *Your beautiful feet are dancing a czardas.*
>
> *Tell me, my God, why am I croaking here?*
> *I curse you, vile Birkenau.*

16. Miklos Nyiszli, *Auschwitz*, trans. Tibere Kremer & Richard Seaver (New York: Fawcett Crest, 1960), p. 99; *From the History of KL Auschwitz* (New York: Howard Fertig, 1982), p. 210.

Feet are dancing, dancing.
Death is lulling me to sleep.

You will go into the fire with me, Maryka.[17]

Eli Pfefferkorn
David H. Hirsch

17. This song is translated from Polish by Roslyn and David H. Hirsch on the basis of a recording made by the late Aleksander Kulisiewicz, in Poland in 1981: *Piesne Obozowe* (Songs of the Camps), Polskie Nagrania: MUZA (SX 1715). Kulisiewicz, who was a prisoner in Sachsenhausen from 1939 to 1945 and an extraordinary figure in his own right, was the foremost collector of camp songs. His archive is now being administered by his son, Krzystof, a student in the faculty of English Linguistics at the Jagiellonian University in Cracow. From what we have seen and heard of these still largely untranslated materials, they are an essential resource for those who wish to understand the survival of the human spirit in the concentration camps.

aktzia

An organized raid by the SS and/or local militias for the purpose of rounding up Jews, either for deportation or to be murdered in the designated places of execution nearby.

blokowa

A female prisoner in charge of a block, translated variously as "block elder," "block leader," "block supervisor," or "block senior." *Blokowy* is the masculine form. Feminine plural is *blokowe*.

blocksperre

A curfew during which prisoners were forbidden to leave the living quarters.

effektenkammer

A warehouse where newly confiscated goods were located.

gimnasium (*gymnasium*)

Polish high school. Completion with a diploma is generally considered equivalent to two years of study in an American college program.

herrenvolk

Master race.

Judenrein (or *Judenfrei*)

The aim of the Nazi Policy vis-à-vis the Jews during this period was to make Germany and German occupied areas free of Jews.

kanada

A branch of the camp where the warehouse containing confiscated goods was located.

kapo

Chief of a work battalion. The chief of a larger group was called an "elder *kapo*" or *oberkapo*. The head of a smaller group was called a *vorarbeiter*. All of these functions were carried out by prisoners.

komando (Polish spelling)

A work battalion.

kozak	In the context used here, a strenuous Russian dance.
lagerälteste	Within the hierarchy of the camp, this was the highest rank that could be attained by a prisoner. Often translated as "camp elder."
läufer	A messenger or courier. Polonized to *lauferka* (feminine singular), *lauferki* (feminine plural).
leichenkomando	Work battalion assigned to bury the dead prisoners.
leichenauto	Hearse.
mussulman	The name given to a camp inmate whose physical condition had deteriorated to the point of no return and who had consequently lost the will to live.
nachtwache	Night shift.
oberkapo	See *kapo*.
obersturmführer	First lieutenant, low ranking officer in the SS.
rapportführer	Non-commissioned officer in charge of roll call.
schreiberka	Clerk, an inmate. Polonization in the feminine of German *schreiber*.
sonderkomando	A work battalion made up of prisoners assigned to work in the gas chambers and crematoria.
sztubowa	The "room elders," "room overseers," or "room leaders," assistants to the *blokowa*, whose job was to maintain order among prisoners. A feminine Polonization of the German *stubendienst* (military term for "orderly").

unionfabrik	Part of the complex of factories in Birkenau.
vorarbeiter	See *kapo*.
zugang	German term for "new arrival." Plural *zugangen*, Polonized to *zugangi*.